SOCIAL ENTERPRISE 2.0

Books by Mike Hamel

The Entrepreneur's Creed: The Principles & Passions of 20 Successful Entrepreneurs (2001)

Executive Influence: Impacting Your Workplace for Christ (2003)

Giving Back: Using Your Influence to Create Social Change (2003)

Stumbling toward Heaven: Mike Hamel on Cancer, Crashes and Questions (2011)

We Will Be Landing Shortly: Now What? (2014)

One World One Standard: The ROW Foundation (2018)

Spencer MacCallum: A Man beyond His Time (2021)

SOCIAL ENTERPRISE 2.0

THE OWP DIFFERENCE

Mike Hamel

Social Enterprise 2.0: The OWP Difference
Copyright © 2021 by EMT Communications, LLC.

Published by EMT Communications, LLC.
All rights reserved. Except for brief quotations in printed reviews, no part of this book may be reproduced in any form without written permission from EMT Communications.

All undocumented dialogue in this book is from personal conversations with the individuals named.

First printing—July 2021

ISBN: 978-0-578-93568-3

Cover design by Chris Kairos / Forefront Brand
Interior design by Niddy Griddy Design, Inc.

*To the men and women who are making the dream of
One World. One Standard.
a reality for thousands—one day to be millions—of people
around the world.
May your tribe increase!*

Contents

Introduction	9
Drug Test	11
ROW Stories: Fatima's Victory	15
1. Roots and Branches	17
2. Big Pharma	31
ROW Stories: The Susan Project	43
3. Dreamer	45
4. Accomplices	57
ROW Stories: Fred's Mission	71
5. Drugs of Choice	73
6. Treatable Disease	85
ROW Stories: Mother and Son	95
7. One World. One Standard.	97
8. No Money, No Mission	111
ROW Stories: Bety's New Chapter	119
9. Minefield	121
10. Social Entrepreneurs	131
ROW Stories: Amanda Award	145
11. Looking Ahead	147
Drug Test Answers	155
Appendix	157
Epilepsy: A Public Health Imperative	
ROW Foundation: Working Toward One World. One Standard.	171
Endnotes	175

Introduction

A social enterprise is an organization that applies commercial strategies to maximize improvements in financial, social, and environmental well-being. Social Enterprise 2.0 (SE 2.0) as used in this book features a for-profit business and a charitable foundation whose symbiotic partnership takes social enterprise to the next level. The SE 2.0 business is committed to making money, but that's not the primary reason for its existence.

Many SE 2.0 adventures start from scratch. Starting a new business is nothing new. More than 543,000 are started every month by entrepreneurs in the US. Scott Boyer is one of those entrepreneurs. He left a lucrative career to launch a high-risk startup. "High-risk" isn't hyperbole. Half of these startups won't survive five years, and only a third will make it beyond ten years.[1] To make it even more challenging, Scott's venture is in the pharmaceutical sector, where entry costs are high and public opinion is low.

In 2017, only 9 percent of Americans believed that pharma and biotech companies put patients before profits.[2] But that's exactly what Scott and his partners set out to do with their new kind of social enterprise: help people and build trust. Returning to the idea stated by the late George W. Merck, "medicine is for the people,"[3] and not just the people in wealthier nations, Scott's hybrid approach can serve as a model for others who want to do well in business while doing good in the world.

Drug Test

This book begins with a self-administered drug test to see what you know about legal drugs and the industry that discovers and dispenses them. No fair checking Google or Wikipedia. The answers are found in the chapters that follow—or on page 155 if you can't wait.

1. The average life span in the US in 1900 was forty-nine. The average life span in 2020, after discoveries such as vaccines, insulin, penicillin, and beta-blockers, is _____.

2. Without this drug, _____, 75 percent of the people now alive would not be alive because their parents or grandparents would have died from infections.

3. How big is the worldwide pharmaceutical industry in US dollars? $_____

4. _____ percent of the global pharmaceutical market is focused on the US, Europe, and Asia.

5. Americans spend more on prescription drugs than anyone else in the world, about $_____ per person annually.

6. _____ percent of Americans take prescription meds.

7. According to Gallup's ratings of US Business and Industry in 2020, which sectors are held in the lowest esteem by Americans?

_____

_____

_____

8. Generic drugs are used to fill _____ percent of prescriptions in the US. Are these generics readily available in low- and middle-income countries? Yes / No

9. _____ billion people living in low- and middle-income countries do not have access to modern medicine.

10. Around _____ million people have epilepsy, with more than _____ new cases every year.

Behind Every Person with Epilepsy, There's a Story

Fatima's Victory
Medical Assistance Sierra Leone

With only two practicing neurologists in Sierra Leone, an estimated 85 percent of people with epilepsy live with untreated seizures. Fatima has had epilepsy since age three. For thirty years the treatment available to her did not control her seizures. She has endured social stigma that impacted her education and livelihood.

Medical Assistance Sierra Leone (MASL) in Sierra Leone sends community health workers to outlying villages to lead epilepsy support groups. Learning she might be able to get help, Fatima made a 150-mile trip to the epilepsy clinic in Freetown run by MASL. She got an EEG (electroencephalogram) and was prescribed Roweepra provided by the ROW Foundation. For the first time in her life, her seizures are under control. Her community is amazed, and her successful treatment may help others understand that epilepsy is a medical disorder, not a spiritual condition, as is commonly believed in some non-Western countries.

Seizure control is an amazing victory for Fatima. But she's still unable to find a job because of mental health issues and social stigmas. Medication is just one weapon, albeit a critical one, in the fight against epilepsy, along with diagnosis, training, and education. MASL developed a children's book to be distributed in schools throughout the country. The ROW Foundation partnered with MASL to deliver ten thousand copies of *Jariatu Has Epilepsy* to Sierra Leone. ROW saw the tremendous potential of this beautifully illustrated story to help children become change agents. With a shortage of textbooks across Africa, it will have a big impact on students while teaching them that those with epilepsy are not to be feared.

1
Roots and Branches

A Short History of Medicine:
2000 BC: "Here, eat this root."
1000 BC: "That root is heathen, say this prayer."
AD 1850: "That prayer is superstition, drink this potion."
AD 1940: "That potion is snake oil, swallow this pill."
AD 1985: "That pill is ineffective, take this antibiotic."
AD 2000: "That antibiotic is artificial. Here, eat this root."
—Author Unknown

Medicines have been around for as long as the plants from which they are derived. They were extracted and used by prehistoric tribes and refined by the ancient Egyptians, who came up with the profession of physician. They developed a cornucopia of drugs for everything from constipation to cancer. Following in their footsteps, the Greeks produced the most famous doctor of antiquity, Hippocrates. He is credited with the idea that the body is composed of four "humors," or liquids. Medicines and procedures such as bloodletting were employed to keep these in balance, which was the key to health.

Engineers and empire builders, the Romans set up hospitals and public health systems. They had a superstar doctor of their own, Galen, who expounded the four humors in his books. Later generations translated these and other medical texts and added insights throughout the Middle Ages, with mixed results. Medicine was often mingled with superstition, a polygamous relationship the scientific revolution would seek to annul.

Not until the nineteenth century did pharmacology come into its own. It had two primary taproots, according to researchers Arthur A. Daemmrich and Mary Ellen Bowden: "apothecaries that moved into wholesale production of drugs such as morphine, quinine, and strychnine in the middle of the 19th century, and dye and chemical companies that established research labs and discovered medical applications for their products starting in the 1880s."[4]

The largest pharmaceutical companies in the world today can trace their heritage back to these beginnings.

Top Tier

The top ten pharma companies by revenue in 2020 were:

1. Johnson & Johnson
2. Roche
3. Novartis
4. Merck & Co.
5. AbbVie
6. GlaxoSmithKline
7. Bristol Myers Squibb
8. Pfizer
9. Sanofi
10. Takeda[5]

The ranking and revenues change from year to year depending on what data is used and what drugs are popular, but the players in the top tier usually remain there. Let's take a brief look at the roots of these companies in somewhat chronological order.

A German apothecary shop founded in 1668 would wind up in the hands of Heinrich Emanuel Merck in 1827. He began making and marketing alkaloids. The company products soon included morphine and cocaine. George Merck immigrated to the US in 1891 and set up what would become Merck & Co. Through a series of mergers and medical firsts—vitamin B1, measles vaccine, statins—Merck grew into one of the world's leading pharmaceutical companies with products such as Keytruda for cancer, Vioxx for arthritis, and lovastatin, the first statin drug.

Takeda Pharmaceuticals was founded in 1781 by thirty-two-year-old Chobei Takeda I. He bought traditional Japanese and Chinese medicines from wholesalers and sold them to local doctors and merchants in Osaka. His company began importing products from other countries around 1895. In 1907 it got exclusive rights to sell products from Bayer, in Japan. It incorporated in 1925 and today is the largest pharmaceutical company in Asia. Its current focus is on gastroenterology, oncology, and plasma-derived therapies.

In an oft-repeated pattern, war greatly benefited the drug business. Edward Robinson Squibb, a naval doctor who served during the Mexican-American War, got so disgusted with the medicines available to him that at one point he threw the stock overboard. After the war he invented an improved method of distilling ether and went on to establish his own laboratory and business in 1858. His medicines were in great demand during the Civil War and beyond. By 1883 he was making and marketing more than 320 products around the world. The company Dr. Squibb left to his sons continued to expand. So did another New York drug business started in 1887 by two friends, William McLaren Bristol and John Ripley Myers. The companies merged a century later to form Bristol Myers Squibb. Its top-selling drugs are Eliquis, Opdivo, and Orencia.

The Civil War also turned the Pfizer chemical company into a thriving concern. Founded in 1849 by two German immigrants, Pfizer supplied the Union Army with vital chemicals and medications. The company grew and by 1880 had become America's leading producer of citric acid used in popular new drinks such as Coca-Cola, Dr Pepper, and Pepsi-Cola. Along the way it acquired the Upjohn Pill and Granule Company, founded in 1886 by Dr. William E. Upjohn. It perfected the large-scale production of cortisone and progesterone. Its best-known drugs are Xanax, Halcion, Motrin, and Rogaine. Upjohn merged with the Sweden-based Pharmacia AB in 1995. Pharmacia AB merged with Pfizer in 2003. Pfizer has been a pioneer in medicines such as penicillin, broad-spectrum antibiotics, and breakthrough products for angina, hypertension, and depression.

English chemist Thomas Beecham opened the world's first factory exclusively devoted to medicines in Lancashire, England, in 1859. His breakout product was the laxative Beecham's Pills. The pills were made until 1998 by Beecham companies, including SmithKline Beecham, which merged with Glaxo Wellcome in 2000 to become GlaxoSmithKline (GSK). Parts of GSK go back to Joseph Nathan and Co. His company, founded in 1873, became Glaxo Laboratories, named after the baby food it made. Burroughs Wellcome & Company was founded in London seven years later, in 1880. Glaxo and Wellcome merged in 1995 to form Glaxo Wellcome, on the way to becoming GSK. GSK products include amoxicillin for bacterial infections, valacyclovir for herpes virus infections, and lamotrigine for epilepsy.

Johnson & Johnson was started in 1886 by three brothers. The company initially made surgical dressings and first-aid kits. It branched into baby powder, feminine hygiene products, and dental floss before the turn of the century and just kept diversifying. It is now the largest pharma conglomerate in the world, with 2020 global revenues topping $82 billion. It has subsidiaries in more than sixty countries focused on pharmaceuticals, medical devices, and consumer health care. Its brands include household names such as Band-Aid, Tylenol, Acuvue contact lenses, Neutrogena skin and beauty products, and Johnson's Baby products.

Two years after the start of Johnson & Johnson, Chicago physician and drug store owner Wallace Calvin Abbott began what would become another pharma juggernaut: Abbott Laboratories. Abbott worked in the back of his store to create more consistent dosages and delivery methods for common drugs such as morphine, quinine, codeine, and strychnine. (As Dr. Peter Mere Latham wryly notes, "Poisons and medicine are oftentimes the same substance given with different intents."[6]) The business expanded to include new drugs, medical devices, and nutritional products. It also branched into other countries. In 2013 Abbott spun off its pharmaceutical business into a global company called AbbVie. Its leading drugs are Imbruvica, Lupron, and Humira, which is used to treat arthritis, psoriasis, and Crohn's disease.

F. Hoffmann-La Roche & Co. got started in Basel, Switzerland, in 1896. La Roche saw the potential of the industrial manufacture of medicines. The company got its first patent and opened branches in other countries. The cough syrup Sirolin was their workhorse. It remained on the market for more than sixty years. Today, Roche Holding

AG oversees the company's two divisions, pharmaceuticals and diagnostics. The pharmaceuticals division makes antibiotics, antimalarials, and chemotherapy drugs.

The Basel region was a center of the textile and dye trades. It became, and remains, a pharmaceutical hub. Almost two-thirds of all employees of the Swiss pharmaceutical trade today work in the area. Three chemical and dye-trading companies that started there in the 1800s—Geigy, Ciba, and Sandoz—eventually merged in the late 1900s into Novartis. It markets a wide range of pharmaceuticals and on the consumer-health side sells popular products such as Excedrin, Ex-Lax, Maalox, and NoDoz.

The French entry into the top tier of pharma firms is Sanofi. It is the product of about fifty acquisitions and mergers—literally—with the oldest companies dating back to the 1800s. One of the predecessors of the modern healthcare conglomerate, it developed medicines for meningitis and diabetes, as well as a wide range of cancer drugs. Its over-the-counter products include Theraflu, Flonase, Contac, and Nicorette.

Two other companies just outside the top ten are well-known to American consumers. German dye salesman Friedrich Bayer and master dyer Johann Friedrich Weskott started Friedr. Bayer et comp. in 1863. When they figured out their dyes had medicinal properties, they expanded into pharmaceuticals. Their big moneymaker around the turn of the century was aspirin. Today they are the twelfth-largest pharma company on the planet.

Ranked at number fifteen is Eli Lilly and Company, started in 1876 by chemist and Union cavalry officer Colonel Eli Lilly. He pioneered innovations such as putting medicines into gelatin capsules for more precise dosing, and adding fruit flavoring and sugarcoating to make pills easier to swallow. In 1917 Lilly's facility in Indianapolis was reputed to be the largest capsule factory in the world. Today its brands include Cialis, Cymbalta, methadone, and Prozac.

When these and the other pharma companies got their start, there wasn't a clear distinction between chemistry, pharmacology, and consumer goods. As health-care journalist Robin Walsh points out, "The unregulated nature of the trade in medicines during this period ensured there was a far less strict delineation between 'pharmaceutical' and 'chemical' industries than we have nowadays. These companies focused as much on cod liver oil, toothpaste, citric acid for soft drinks, and hair gel as on prescription medicines, as well as selling products like heroin on the over-the-counter market."[7]

Vitamins and Vaccines

Pharmaceutical companies established two new categories of products in the twentieth century: vitamins and vaccines. These advancements improved human health and increased corporate profits.

People have always known that plants and food contained health-promoting properties, but individual micronutrients weren't discovered until 1910. They were dubbed "vitamins" two years later. The thirteen "essential" vitamins we know today were identified between 1910 and 1948. Commercial sales began in the 1930s. It would take another twenty years for inexpensive vitamin supplements to become popular.

Vitamins aren't classified as drugs but as dietary supplements. The Food and Drug Administration (FDA) views them as food, not pharmaceuticals. But pharmaceutical companies are dominant players in the supplement market, which is expected to more than double from $133 billion in 2016 to $272.4 billion by 2028. The supplement industry in the US was worth $42.6 billion in 2019, with the average American spending $56 a month on dietary supplements alone.

The history of vaccines in the Western world goes back to 1796, when an English doctor, Edward Jenner, came up with the smallpox vaccine. (There were versions of vaccines in China and Africa long before then.) It's impossible to calculate how many people died from the disease through the ages, but smallpox killed more than 300 million people in the twentieth century alone. No one dies of smallpox today because of vaccinations.

It would be almost a century after Jenner that chemist Louis Pasteur would develop the next major vaccine, this one for rabies, in 1885. From the new science of bacteriology pioneered by Pasteur in France and Robert Koch in Germany would come vaccines against polio, diphtheria, tetanus, anthrax, cholera, typhoid, tuberculosis, and more. Researchers also created vaccines for childhood diseases such as measles, mumps, and rubella, greatly reducing infant and child mortality. In the mid-1900s, polio was the leading cause of disability in the US, but the introduction of a polio vaccine in 1955 has eradicated the disease here, and efforts are underway to do the same worldwide.

Biologist Leonard Hayflick helped make human vaccines widely available. He ardently believes "there is no medication, lifestyle change, public health innovation, or medical procedure ever developed that has even come close to the life-saving, life-extending, and primary prevention benefits associated with vaccines."[8]

As detailed by Walter Isaacson in his book *The Code Breaker: Jennifer Doudna, Gene Editing, and the Future of the Human Race*:

Throughout human history, we have been subjected to wave after wave of viral and bacterial plagues. The first known one was the Babylon flu epidemic around 1200 BC. The plague of Athens in 429 BC killed close to 100,000 people, the Antonine plague in the second century killed ten million, the plague of Justinian in the sixth century killed fifty million, and the Black Death of the fourteenth century took almost 200 million lives, close to half of Europe's population. The COVID pandemic that killed more than 1.5 million people in 2020 will not be the final plague. However, thanks to the new RNA vaccine technology, our defenses against most future viruses are likely to be immensely faster and more effective.[9]

The number of COVID deaths had doubled by May 2021; the actual numbers are no doubt higher. Unique vaccines were quickly created and fast-tracked to market. "Never before had an RNA vaccine been approved for use," Isaacson notes:

> But a year after the novel coronavirus was first identified, both Pfizer/BioNTech and Moderna had devised these new genetic vaccines and tested them in large clinical trials, involving people like me, where they proved more than 90 percent effective. . . . The invention of easily reprogrammable RNA vaccines was a lightning-fast triumph of human ingenuity, but it was based on decades of curiosity-driven research into one of the most fundamental aspects of life on planet earth: how genes encoded by DNA are transcribed into snippets of RNA that tell cells what proteins to assemble.[10]

Magic Pills and Biotech

Other major breakthroughs in the 1900s increased the importance of pharmaceuticals in daily life. Frederick Banting discovered insulin to treat diabetes in 1921, which Eli Lilly mass-produced and marketed. And Alexander Fleming's discovery of penicillin in 1928 revolutionized medicine—and the world. During World War II, eleven companies worked on penicillin under the auspices of the War Production Board. "The immense scale and sophistication of the penicillin development effort marked a new era for the way the pharmaceutical industry developed drugs," observes Walsh. "[And] as the industry grew wealthy thanks to its growing portfolio of products, the potential ethical conflicts of making money from selling healthcare products became increasingly apparent."[11]

The growing portfolio of life-improving products would include the birth control pill (1960), ibuprofen (1961), beta-blockers to treat angina (1962), Valium (1963), cyclosporine, the first effective immunosuppressive drug (1970), and ACE inhibitors (1975). The ulcer medication Tagamet (1977) became the first $1 billion-a-year drug. Antiviral drugs started to appear in 1979. Prozac, the first selective serotonin reuptake inhibitor (SSRI), came out in 1987, the same year Merck marketed the first commercial statin—lovastatin.

Along with these new drugs came a whole new way of doing pharmacology and bioscience that ushered in the biotech boom. The global biotech market is expected to top $775 billion by 2025 according to research by Global Market Insights.[12] Many companies sold off their chemical and consumer goods businesses and focused on inventing molecules they could own, this in the wake of a 1980 Supreme Court ruling that genetically manipulated organisms could be patented.

The term *biotechnology* was coined in 1919 by Hungarian agricultural engineer Karl Ereky. Biotech therapy, or "biologics," includes any medicine made with or derived from living organisms. In an article titled "Big Biotech Is Here—and It's Starting to Look a Lot Like Big Pharma," Meghana Keshavan gives this helpful clarification:

> Traditionally, the term "biotech" referred to a company that tinkered with biological building blocks to make drugs, for instance by genetically engineering proteins. Pharmaceutical companies, on the other hand, focused on medicinal chemistry, screening huge libraries of compounds to find those that might prove useful at fighting disease. In the last decade or so, this line has been increasingly blurred. Many pharma companies now work on manufacturing drugs inside living cells and "biotech" has become a catchall phrase for startup companies working on all manner of drugs and medical devices.[13]

Going Generic

The rise of generics became a game changer for pharma in the latter half of the twentieth century. Congress passed the Hatch-Waxman Act, also known as the Drug Price Competition and Patent Term Restoration Act, in 1984. It established government regulations for generic drugs and blew the pharmaceutical industry wide open. The number of generics grew dramatically. Before then, only 35 percent of top-selling drugs had generic versions on the market. Almost all do now, as soon as their patents expire, which has caused prices—and margins—to shrink on many medicines.

The FDA defines a *generic drug* as "a medication created to be the same as an already marketed brand-name drug in dosage form, safety, strength, route of administration, quality, performance characteristics, and intended use."[14] While the active ingredients must be the same, trademark laws require that it can't look the same as the brand-name drug. Generics are cheaper because manufacturers don't have to spend millions on developing the drug, taking it through clinical trials, and introducing it to the public. And when more than one company can make the medicine, competition drives prices down. Today nearly nine out of ten prescriptions are filled with generics.

The FDA generally gives patented drugs twenty years of protection, with a total monopoly on sales during that period. Patent holders can try to extend this by slightly modifying the drug or its delivery system, or by combining it with a similar drug. These delaying tactics eventually run their course and generics hit the market, with dramatic impact. According to the IMARC Group, the global generic drug market is projected to grow from $386 billion in 2020 to $517 billion by 2026.[15]

While the generic market is growing, delay tactics by patent holders and low profit margins have decreased competition. The FDA says less than a third of approved generics are being actively marketed. Drugs with less competition and those used by fewer people often see steep price hikes. More than 300 of 1,441 generic drugs had at least one extraordinary price increase over a five-year period according to a 2016 report from the Government Accountability Office (GAO).[16]

Generics have been a blessing for consumers but a challenge for many pharmaceutical companies because of their negative impact on the bottom line. "The industry's focus increased on marketing to maintain market share, on lobbying politicians to protect commercial interests, and on lawyers to enforce legal claims on intellectual property rights," notes Walsh. "These activities have brought a greater suspicion of the industry in the public at large."[17]

"Suspicion" may be too weak a word for how the majority of Americans feel about Big Pharma.

2
Big Pharma

Medicine is for the patient.
Medicine is for the people.
It is not for the profits.
—George W. Merck

"Big Pharma" is the street name for the largest pharmaceutical companies in the world. They sink billions into research, spend billions on marketing, and scoop up billions in sales. There are conflicting figures from different sources, but the stats marshaled by Keith Speights for the Motley Fool in 2018 are representative. He cites some astounding numbers:

- *$1.05 trillion*: global pharmaceutical market revenues
- *$515 billion*: pharmaceutical market revenues from the US and Canada—around half the global total, this from two countries that make up only 7 percent of the world's population
- *21 percent*: the 2015 profit margin that *Forbes* estimated for the health-care technology industry, making it by far the most profitable industry of all[18]

These numbers have only grown since then. Today, Big Pharma employs more than five and a half million people worldwide. More than two million of them are associated with the International Federation of Pharmaceutical Manufacturers & Associations. IFPMA takes its share of credit for the better quality of life we enjoy:

> The research-based biopharmaceutical industry is one of the most innovative sectors in the world, which over the past century has played a unique role in developing new and improved medicines and vaccines to prevent and treat diseases. It is also thanks to biopharmaceutical innovation that societies were able to thrive into through full and healthy lives. This is a unique industry. This uniqueness is even more accentuated as the entire planet is looking for solutions to tackle COVID-19.[19]

Our lives have been made significantly better through pharmacology. A WebMD article, "The 10 Most Important Drugs," recounts the mind-boggling benefits of drugs like penicillin: "As the first antibiotic, it pointed the way to the treatment of microbial disease. Without penicillin, 75% of the people now alive would not be alive because their parents or grandparents would have succumbed to infections."[20]

The first hormone therapy drug, insulin, improved the lives of millions of diabetics. It paved the way for all other hormone-replacement therapies. Ether, the initial drug used as an anesthetic, softened the horrors of surgery. Who doesn't prefer one of its more modern counterparts to a shot of whiskey and a stick to bite on? Other pain-management drugs, such as morphine, have alleviated untold suffering (while also causing a fair amount of it through addiction). Morphine was the forerunner of several generations of pain-killing drugs. Aspirin is at the other end of the potency scale, but it has perhaps relieved more pain in more people than any other medicine.

Pharmacology plays a significant role in the quality and quantity of life. Life expectancy in the US in 1900 was forty-nine years. A century later it's approaching eighty. But along the way, we've become dependent on drugs. The National Center for Health Statistics reports, "In 2015–2016, 45.8% of the U.S. population used prescription drugs in the past 30 days."[21] The price tag: $507.9 billion in 2019.[22] Americans pay more for medications than anyone else because drug prices aren't regulated as in other countries. Manufacturers can charge whatever they want, which has resulted in huge price increases in recent years.

People don't question the core benefits provided by Big Pharma, or its right to make a decent profit. It's the criminal behavior and blatant profiteering of some in the industry that have given pharma a bad reputation. The Gallup Poll's annual trust ranking lists twenty-five Business and Industry sectors in the US. Only three had a negative trust ranking in 2020: the sports industry had a −10, the pharmaceutical industry a −15, and the federal government a −20.[23]

Big Pharma's response to the pandemic has brought a much-needed boost to their reputation. "We have seen a significant uptick in the reputation of the pharmaceutical industry as a result of the actions they've taken through the pandemic," said life sciences expert Greg Rotz. "Collaborations, innovations, additional investments have all gone a long way to help remind society about the importance of innovative medicines to tackle catastrophic disease."[24]

Driving Force

In 2020, *Pharmaceutical Processing World* reported that "26 pharmaceutical companies paid some $33 billion in fines during the 13-year period [2003–2016]. . . . 85% of the pharmaceutical companies sampled had received financial penalties between 2003 and 2016. . . . Pricing violations were the most common reason for fines. In all, there were 78 total fines among the 26 companies related to overpricing drugs reimbursed by the government, fraudulent billing, underpaying rebate obligations and other pricing offenses."[25]

Some pharma companies faced criminal prosecution and paid enormous penalties despite spending more to lobby Congress than any other industry. In 2020, the pharmaceuticals and health products industry spent about $306.23 million on lobbying, more than twice as much as the insurance industry ($151.85 million).[26]

These fines may seem high, but they are paltry compared to the profits made by the drugs at issue. As noted by the watchdog group Public Citizen, "In one case, GSK paid $3 billion for violations involving multiple drugs, three of which netted them $28 billion in sales during the time covered by the settlement. In another, Johnson & Johnson was fined $2 billion in 2013 for violations involving Risperdal, among other drugs. But Risperdal alone earned about that amount every year for the first 12 years after it went on the market."[27]

The driving force behind most criminal and unethical activity is money. Martin Shkreli drew the nation's ire when his startup company, Turing Pharmaceuticals, acquired Daraprim, a drug used to treat life-threatening infections. He promptly raised the price from $13.50 to $750 a tablet, a 5,000 percent increase.

A few months later, at the Forbes Healthcare Summit,

Shkreli said, "I could have raised it higher and made more profits for our shareholders, which is my primary duty. No one wants to say it. No one's proud of it. But this is a capitalist society. Capitalist system. Capitalist rules. And my investors expect me to maximize profits. Not to minimize them or go half or go 70 percent. But to go to 100 percent of the profit curve."[28]

Nirmal Mulye, CEO of Nostrum Laboratories, would agree. As reported by *Financial Times*: "[The] Missouri-based drugmaker more than quadrupled the price of a bottle of nitrofurantoin from $474.75 to $2,392.... In an interview, Nirmal Mulye, Nostrum chief executive, said he had priced the product according to market dynamics, adding: 'I think it is a moral requirement to make money when you can…to sell the product for the highest price.'"[29]

Obscene price increases in essential medications are all too common. "Top executives at Mylan, the pharmaceutical company that owns EpiPen, reportedly raked in nearly $300 million in compensation from 2011 to 2015," Time.com disclosed. "The fat payoffs rolled in during a period when the list prices for EpiPens soared, increasing over 500% in about a decade. Today, EpiPens, which cost Mylan around $30 to produce, go for over $600 before coupons or rebates."[30] At least some of the profits went to Mylan's chairman and former CEO Robert Coury's pay package for 2016—$98 million.

Reasons or Excuses

The pharmaceutical industry spent $186 billion on research and development in 2019. Costs are expected to climb to more than $230 billion by 2026. Around 17,700 prescription drugs were in the 2020 R&D pipeline. Big Pharma claims the cost of developing new products can be as high as $1.5 billion per drug. However, some experts estimate the actual cost is closer to $60 million.

Whatever the true cost, it's often not a factor in the market price. As seen with Valeant, many companies acquire drugs for which they haven't spent a dime on R&D and turbo-boost the price. A Yale study on Curbing Unfair Drug Prices concludes that,

> high drug prices are forcing some patients to skip doses of critical medicines, and others to choose between their health and necessities like food and rent. Meanwhile, the pharmaceutical industry continues to launch new drugs at exorbitant prices, increase prices of many old drugs without justification, and reap record profits.
>
> Evidence has unequivocally shown that high drug prices are not linked to the actual costs of research, development, and manufacturing. Instead, inflated drug prices are a result of drug manufacturers' power to charge whatever price the market will bear.[31]

"Half of the scientifically innovative drugs approved in the U.S. from 1998 to 2007 resulted from research at universities and biotech firms, not big drug companies," says Ethan Rome in his *HuffPost* blog. "And despite their rhetoric, drug companies spend 19 times more on marketing than on research and development."[32]

Another justification for the big sticker price on essential drugs is downstream savings. Gilead Sciences, marketer of the hepatitis C drug Sovaldi, justified its $1,000-per-pill price by citing the downstream savings of preventing complications. "Imagine if the same approach had been used for the polio vaccine or penicillin," says Dr. Kenneth L. Davis, CEO of the Mount Sinai Health System. "These essential medicines would have been unaffordable for much of society. Indeed, a US Senate study found Gilead Sciences knew a lower price would allow more patients to be treated."[33]

A third rationalization offered by Big Pharma for big prices is that nobody pays them. Kaleo Pharma is singled out in a 2017 *Los Angeles Times* article by David Lazarus. He explains how in response to the opioid crisis, Kaleo jacked up the list price for its Evzio auto-injector—used to save people who overdose on painkillers—by 600 percent. Kaleo CEO Spencer Williamson responded, "Although the list price for Evzio is more than $4,000, that's not a true net price to anyone . . . due to numerous discounts and rebates that are negotiated in the supply chain that make up our healthcare system."[34]

"In other words," Lazarus quips, "even though the price tag for his company's easy-to-use, lifesaving device is ridiculous and indefensible, there's no need to worry because backroom deals by assorted players in the healthcare food chain make that price tag meaningless. And that, in a nutshell, illustrates the lunacy of the US healthcare system." Lazarus explains:

> Most other developed nations place limits on how much drug companies can charge to prevent them from taking advantage of the sick. A fair profit is fine. Price gouging is not. In this country, drugmakers charge whatever they can get away with, which perhaps would be tolerable if we had an efficient, transparent marketplace in which patients benefit from robust competition and an ability to shop

around for the best price. But we don't. Often, we have a single provider of a drug or medical technology that, thanks to its monopoly power, is in a position to profit handsomely from people's misfortune.[35]

That "monopoly power" leads to avarice is evident when comparing drug prices in other countries. As Tim Wu notes in the *New York Times*: "Daraprim, the antiparasitic drug whose price was raised by Mr. Shkreli to nearly $750 per pill, sells for a little more than $2 overseas. The cancer drug Cosmegen is priced at $1,400 or more per injection here, as opposed to about $20 to $30 overseas."[36] Popular drugs such as Opdivo (Bristol-Myers Squibb) and Keytruda (Merck) are available in China for half what they cost in the US.

Middlemen

In addition to the profits made by drug manufacturers, there are middlemen who add huge markups when moving product from the factory to the patient through the pharmacy. Chief among them are wholesalers and pharmacy benefits managers (PBMs). About one-third of all drug spending in the US goes to these middlemen, according to an analysis published by Health Affairs.

Wholesalers buy, store, and distribute medications and serve as "inventory control points." Three wholesalers dominate this space. AmerisourceBergen, Cardinal Health, and McKesson account for about 90 percent of all revenues from drug distribution in the US. Their combined estimated revenues for 2017 topped $424 billion.[37]

Then there are the PMBs. PBMs review and pay claims and negotiate discounts and rebates with manufacturers. The three largest players control 80 percent of the market: Express Scripts, CVS Caremark, and Optum Rx. Pharmacies must be included in these big networks to survive. PBMs make unparalleled profits in several ways, according to Scott Knoer, chief pharmacy officer of the Cleveland Clinic. These include rebate negotiations, spread (the difference between what a PBM collects from the payer and what it pays the pharmacy), exclusivity agreements (forcing patients to use pharmacies owned by the PBM), and direct and indirect remuneration fees.

And then there are the hospitals. In a move to share some of the blame for high prices, PhRMA commissioned a study by the Moran Company, which "found that almost one in five of the 3,792 hospitals studied upcharge patients and insurers for medicine by 700%. The majority of hospitals (83%) asked for more than double of the medicine's original cost, and 53% of facilities marked up drugs between 200% and 400%. Just 2% had a markup range under 100% and, on average, hospitals charged 479% of their cost for drugs nationwide."[38]

Manufacturers, wholesalers, PBMs, and hospitals all stand accused of putting profits before people. The heads of the leading wholesalers were summoned before Congress to face charges of criminal misconduct for their role in the opioid crisis. The CDC reported that nearly 500,000 people died from opioid overdoses between 1999 and 2019. The *Washington Post* reported:

> The fight over who is accountable for the epidemic has led to the largest civil case in U.S. history and involves nearly two dozen major drug companies. The 2,500 cases from around the nation have been consolidated in U.S. District Court in Cleveland. In October [2017], several drug companies reached a $260 million settlement with two counties in Ohio.

Johnson & Johnson, which owned two companies that processed and imported raw material to manufacture oxycodone, reached its own settlement. The remaining cases are pending.

Purdue Pharma, the drug manufacturer accused of triggering the nation's epidemic through its sale of OxyContin, filed for bankruptcy in September 2019.[39]

Litigation and appeals continue, and the price tag in human lives and criminal fines will only escalate.

Change at the Top

During the decade in which the opioid crisis unfolded, John Hammergren, former CEO of McKesson, received $639 million in compensation. His 2017 earnings amounted to $97.6 million. McKesson is one of three distributors currently negotiating an $18 billion payment for their role in the crisis.

Big Pharma has fallen a long way from the days when George Merck, one of its pioneers, said: "We try never to forget that medicine is for the people. It is not for the profits. The profits follow, and if we have remembered that, they have never failed to appear."[40]

Hammergren and other pharma CEOs make a lot of money. AXIOS crunched the numbers and reported that the CEOs of 177 health-care companies collectively made $2.6 billion in 2018. Their salaries aren't necessarily out of line with other Fortune 500 CEOs, but they represent a change at the top of pharmaceutical companies, as noted by Dr. Kenneth Davis:

> Doctors take the Hippocratic Oath, pledging to uphold ethical standards in treating patients, which includes

prescribing and administering medicines. Time was when the majority of pharmaceutical company CEOs were doctors and scientists. The implicit social contract by which they conducted business was clear: in return for a free market, drugs would be affordable. But today's CEOs have a very different set of values than the past leaders of their companies. Doctors and scientists have been replaced, and their core values of improving health for all have been lost. This new generation of leaders clearly does not feel compelled to abide by the moral imperative inherent in the ethical drug business. Rather than feeling bound by a social contract with patients, their dedication is to stockholders. So they employ pricing strategies designed to maximize profits.[41]

There's an inherent tension in business between enriching oneself and helping others. How this tension is managed is the difference between many CEOs of Big Pharma and social entrepreneurs like the one you're about to meet.

The Susan Project
Purple Bench Initiative

Helping people achieve their potential is a powerful thing. Those people with epilepsy in low-income countries face a wide range of challenges. ROW partner Purple Bench Initiative (PBI) addresses the stigma associated with epilepsy in Uganda.

Susan is very bright and dreams of becoming a doctor someday. However, her epilepsy has created multiple physical and economic hurdles. Due to a seizure, she fell onto an open flame while cooking. In addition, she had to breathe dangerous smoke while cooking, and collecting water required a three-kilometer walk. Still in her teenage years, Susan was also the victim of ongoing social stigma that often surrounds people with epilepsy.

The Susan Project was launched by PBI to help Susan and to create community awareness regarding epilepsy.

Adults and children teamed up to dig a rainwater collection tank and build a stove that protects Susan from flames and smoke. Camaraderie with her community during the project boosted Susan's self-esteem. PBI founder Nina Mago held an awareness session to explain that epilepsy is a medical condition. It is neither contagious nor a result of evil spirits. Susan was also paired with Maria, a caring community health worker who is now her mentor. PBI arranged a hospital visit for Susan, and new medication has her seizures under control.

Money from ROW allowed Purple Bench to impact Susan and her community and to create a model for future programs to help Ugandan families affected by epilepsy.

3
Dreamer

*The best way to make your dreams come true
is to wake up.*
—Paul Valéry

S cott Boyer is a man on a mission. He's not hyper, just keenly focused, with a ready smile and intense eyes. He balances his sixty-to-eighty-hour workweeks with regular time in the gym, on the bike, or skiing when he can get away to Colorado. He stands six foot one and keeps his weight at 190 pounds. His father died at fifty-eight due to poor health, and Scott is determined to stick around much longer than that to see his dream become reality.

Born in Sioux City, Iowa, in 1959, Scott was the middle of five children. His mother, Bernice, was a stay-at-home mom. His father, Vern, ran a successful business in the meat industry. "Boyer's Provisions was an Oscar Mayer sort of operation," Scott recalls. "We made hot dogs, polish sausage, smokies, ham, bacon. Nothing better than eating meat right out of a smokehouse, unless you're a vegetarian. It was a family business, and we all worked hard. If I wanted money, Dad would say, 'Come down to the plant and I'll pay you six dollars an hour.' Six dollars an hour; I'm there! That strong work ethic definitely shaped who I am."

After high school Scott went to nearby Morningside College, attending classes Monday, Wednesday, and Friday, and working at Boyer's on Tuesday and Thursday. He lived at home to save money. Tragedy struck a few years after Scott graduated when his dad died of a sudden heart attack. Unprepared to run the business, the family sold it and the children moved on to different jobs.

With BS degrees in business and psychology, Scott went to work for a health-care purchasing group. His involvement with hospitals and elder-care facilities gave him insight into where the money was, and an idea of where to head careerwise: pharmaceuticals.

Abbott, Bristol, InVentiv

Scott joined Abbott Laboratories, a multibillion-dollar health-care conglomerate, in 1985. Only the year before, Abbott had received FDA approval of the first test to identify the HIV virus. Business was booming on several fronts. He started as a sales representative for the pharmaceutical division with a territory that included parts of Iowa, Nebraska, South Dakota, and Minnesota. By this time he had met and married Ruth Cleveringa. Their daughter, Sara, came along in 1988, followed by son Brett in 1990.

Scott excelled at sales and won numerous awards. In 1990, he and his young family moved to Libertyville, Illinois, where he became a sales trainer. A year later he was promoted to district manager. He did well enough to garner several All-Star awards, given to the top 10 percent of the sales force.

In an upward career move, Scott left Abbott for Bristol-Myers Squibb in May 1997. He started as an associate director of regional operations, which entailed a move to the Chicago suburb of Naperville. By the following January, he'd been promoted to regional business director for hospital products. Over the next fifteen years he managed multimillion-dollar promotional and operational budgets as well as the neuroscience business across as many as eighteen states. He played a lead role in multiple expansions and handled successful rollouts of numerous branded drugs. He recruited, hired, trained, evaluated, and managed sales teams of up to 120 people.

"There were two major cardiovascular drugs I worked with during my first years at BMS," Scott recalls. "Pravachol, developed by Sankyo in Japan, was a first-generation statin used to prevent heart disease. We had acquired the rights to sell it in the US. The year Pravachol lost its patent protection [2006], the drug had revenues of $1.3 billion in the US."

The second cardiovascular drug Scott handled was even bigger. Plavix was a blood thinner used to prevent stroke, heart attack, and other heart problems. "It was a phenomenal drug for patients and for the company," Scott explains. "It was the second-best selling drug in the world for years before going off-patent in 2012. It had more than $9 billion in global sales in 2010 alone."

During his tenure with Bristol, Scott also helped manage Abilify, an antipsychotic medication prescribed for schizophrenia, bipolar disorder, and depression. It was one of the world's top-selling drugs before it went off-patent, and Scott contributed to its phenomenal success. Abilify earned annual revenues ranging from $300 million to more than $1 billion. On the Forbes list of best-selling drugs from 1996 through 2012, Abilify was number 12, with almost $42 billion in sales. Plavix ranked number 2, with lifetime sales of $74.7 billion.

Scott was at the top of his game in a very profitable and highly competitive field. He had a salary in the solid six figures and other perks to show for it. He enjoyed being in pharmaceuticals. "I loved my job. When I started in the industry and we came out with a new drug, it would cost $50 or $100 a month. The medicines weren't that expensive, especially compared to today, and most people could afford them. I felt like we were helping people, improving their quality of life, literally saving lives."

But as drug pricing got out of control, he began to have second thoughts. Was this really what he wanted to do with his life? There had to be something more. "I told Ruth, 'This is not the reason I was put on this earth.' But she said, 'Well, for the next few years, it *is* why you were put on this earth. You have to pay for our kids' education. After [they finish] college you can chase your dream, if you still have it. But until then, stay put.'"

Scott did stay put for a few more years, but he noticed rough waters ahead. Many of the products he handled were transitioned to another company, and Abilify was going off-patent in 2015. "I knew I would have to find another spot at Bristol or take a severance package. I decided to take the severance package and get my retirement set. It would give me a safety net so I could try something new. If it worked out, great. If it didn't, at least I would still have my retirement."

In 2012, Scott left BMS and took a job as executive director of business development with InVentiv Health Incorporated, one of the largest contract sales and research organizations in the country. He wanted to gain broader experience. "InVentiv did analysis on companies and products currently on the market or ready to be launched," Scott says. "We did detailed evaluations on their sales potential. Would a drug be a $100 million product or a $1 billion product?"

As he became familiar with the data, he noticed something that piqued his interest. "On the pie charts and graphs, the most common markets were the US, Japan, and the wealthier countries in Europe. China and India might be included sometimes. The other 170 or 180 countries would be lumped together in the last column, always the smallest, and titled ROW—Rest of World. I later learned the term was fairly common in international business. You focus on the major markets, where profits are the greatest, and throw everyplace else into a big bucket, and that's ROW."

It slowly dawned on Scott that practically all drugs were sold in wealthier countries and almost none went to countries in the ROW column. Patent-protected medications nearly never made it to poorer countries, and getting generic medications into them had its own hurdles.

It became harder to overlook or rationalize that most disorders and diseases that could be easily treated by available and inexpensive medications went untreated. The cost to human life and human potential in these situations seemed staggering and inexcusable.

The situation has improved since then, but even by 2020 more than two billion people living in low- and middle- income countries didn't have access to modern medicine because as Zulf Masters, CEO of Masters Speciality Pharma, says, "Big pharma invariably lives in the first world, and first tier countries still offer the lion's share of their revenue stream."[42]

The Access to Medicine Foundation tracks access to medicine around the world. The foundation's executive director, Jayasree Iyer, says, "Compared with ten years ago, pharmaceutical companies are taking seriously the problems people face in low- and middle-income countries when accessing healthcare. The situation is still fragile—a retreat by one company, or a drop in healthcare investments, will jeopardise the progress made so far."[43]

A Whisper

"I began to hear a 'whisper' to do something about ROW, recalls Scott, "to find a way to equalize the graph when it came to medical care. This stirred my sense of justice. I couldn't accept so many people around the world being left behind. It says a lot about us as humans if we've developed cures and treatments for diseases but consciously or unconsciously choose not to deliver them to all those in need. Their futures could be radically changed by a pill that costs a nickel! We had the medications, but we didn't have a way to distribute them. I began to think how tough it would be to live in a ROW country if I had a disease I knew could be inexpensively treated with medications to which I had no access."

Scott knew the feeling of being disadvantaged through no fault of his own. In his case, a birth defect. "People seldom notice it now, but I was born with only one ear. I had a butch haircut until the seventh grade, and you can imagine what school was like. The best thing I had going for me was that my older brother was the biggest kid in school. If anybody picked on me, Big Randy would track them down and warn them to leave me alone. Because of his size, they did. I've reflected on this the last few years. Perhaps in some small way my childhood experience gives me an affinity with people who are suffering because of circumstances beyond their control."

Still, as a businessman, Scott understood the logic

behind the social injustice. "Big Pharma does a lot of great things," he readily admits. "But in the end they are for-profit corporations, accountable to their shareholders. Their goal is to create useful products and then to maximize profits. Inexpensive medications that could save millions of lives don't get to the people who need them in underdeveloped regions because profits are too low."

Scott's time with InVentiv provided not only an incentive to try something different, but also the education to pull it off. "InVentiv taught me a lot about distribution, contracting, human resources, market access, and other aspects of the business. I got a better understanding of pharma operations from top to bottom rather than just from a marketing perspective. This knowledge gave me more confidence to start a company of my own."

But leaving the pinnacle of a lucrative career for a high-risk startup made about as much sense as hang gliding, and would be about as dicey. "When I would bring up the topic, Ruth would remind me of our responsibilities and encourage me to wait," Scott says. "She has a deep love for people. She spent her working life as a nurse. She's very involved in church and charitable causes, so her concerns about the financial risk of starting a business weren't selfish but practical. She was right, which is why I kept my day job until our kids finished college."

Bruce, Bob, Ruth

Scott and Ruth attended a church in their neighborhood where they met Bruce and Judy Duncan. Bruce was a few years older, with short, graying hair and wire-rimmed glasses. The couples got to know each other, and when Scott learned Bruce was a CPA with a law degree and decades of business experience, he asked Bruce for help in setting up a not-for-profit foundation. In early December 2013 they met for lunch to discuss the details.

Scott had gotten to know Bruce and felt comfortable sharing his developing vision. For his part, Bruce saw Scott's becoming an expert in pharmaceuticals as having a higher purpose. He told Scott to use that expertise to address social and medical injustices around the world. And he even had a model of how this could be done.

"Scott shared his concept of a pharmaceutical company that would sell branded generics in the US," Bruce remembers, "and a foundation that would use the profits to provide those meds to the rest of the world. I knew a structure that would work best for this idea. Tyndale House Publishing in nearby Carol Stream had started a foundation that owned stock in the for-profit business. The foundation got dividends that it used for philanthropic purposes."

The novel arrangement immediately intrigued Scott.

And Bruce. "At this point in my life I was looking for something meaningful to do. I asked Scott if I could join him, and he said, 'I'd love you to.'"

Bruce reached out to Chuck Stair, a longtime friend, who happened to be chairman of the board of Tyndale. Chuck put Bruce in touch with Tyndale's CFO. "I had a meeting with him, and he gave me the secret sauce," Bruce says. "It had to do with the creation and allocation of stock. Scott and I used that information to set up our hybrid model. In February 2014 we incorporated Wheaton Pharmaceuticals, a for-profit business. We changed the name a few times and settled on OWP Pharmaceuticals. A few months later we registered the not-for-profit ROW Foundation in Illinois."

Before this, Bruce had given Scott a copy of *Halftime: Changing Your Game Plan from Success to Significance*, by Bob Buford. After reading it, Scott signed up for the next

Halftime seminar. Halftime is an organization founded by Buford, former chairman of Buford Television. It helps business and professional leaders move from success to significance. It functions with a Christian worldview and focuses on social entrepreneurs.

According to Buford, one factor catalyzing the social entrepreneurial movement has been a shift in the concept of success: "Success in America has usually been defined in terms of money, fame, and power. Most adults allocate 90 percent of their energies to these Big Three on the 'Success Scale.' What drives a person to become a social entrepreneur is seeing the shallowness of this materialistic value system and switching to the 'Significance Scale,' which is calibrated to serving others instead of self."[44]

An important part of making the switch is operating out of your own history. "I seldom meet a social entrepreneur (SE) whose success hasn't grown out of his or her prior history," Buford writes. "One reason for the tremendous impact of the latest class of SEs is that they're not leaving behind their business skill-sets when they cross over to the social sector. They see a social or spiritual opportunity and organize themselves in a businesslike way to address the challenge."

This idea of building on a lifetime of experience and doing what you do well for the benefit of others resonated with Scott. He realized he could take his lifetime of learning and use it as a platform to move from success to significance. "My strength is in the pharmaceutical industry," he says. "More specifically in strategic planning and commercializing products. That's where I spent my career and where I could have the most impact in the second half of life. I was eager for guidance. I needed encouragement to walk in faith that God would provide the right people and wisdom at the appropriate time. My Halftime experience gave me that. It also connected me to a life coach named Jim Dean, who was a great help."

"For most people I talked to at Halftime, they're not sure about what God is calling them to do next," Jim says. "They may have some ideas, but are just exploring several things. Scott was unusual in that he had real clarity about what he felt God was calling him to do. He didn't need coaching on the business side; he had good experience with that. We focused on the personal side of taking this journey.

"I've worked with a lot of entrepreneurs," Jim continues, "and I'm always fascinated by their business model—what they're going to do and how do they expect to make it work. When Scott told me about his ideas for OWP, I'd never seen a model like that. It was certainly very unusual, but I thought a great model."

Then there was the nonprofit side of Scott's vision, what would become the ROW Foundation.

"I have got a lot of experience working with nonprofits," Jim adds. "One of the biggest challenges is providing ongoing income in order to do what they want to accomplish. Scott's idea of having a business that provided a reliable income stream for the nonprofit was a creative way to do it."

Ruth wasn't very excited about Scott going to Halftime. "I was afraid of what it might do to his life." Her fear turned out to be well-founded, and her anxiety increased when Scott told her sometime later he planned to resign from InVentiv. "Such a big turn for our family," she recalls. "All of a sudden my husband would be unemployed and I'd be the one shouldering the responsibility while he chased his dream. I was working full-time and not the happiest camper. Before this, my job had been a release for me. Now it was something I had to do. But when the pieces started coming together and OWP actually became something real, my attitude changed. Because of the courage I saw in Scott, I could be a little more courageous in my faith."

"Ruth's heart has impacted me for the more than thirty years we've been married," Scott says. "She's a very giving person. She's influenced me to be more giving. I could have been a coldhearted, bloodthirsty pharmaceutical executive except that living with her made me think about people differently. OWP would not exist without her."

Skin in the Game

The concept of "skin in the game" may go back to Shakespeare's *The Merchant of Venice*, where Antonio has to put up a pound of flesh as collateral on a loan. It means to have a personal stake or significant risk in a venture.

When it came time to put up or shut up, Scott and Ruth were still at opposite ends of the spectrum. She focused on security. He was more concerned with missed opportunity. Their daughter, Sara, had graduated from Purdue in 2011 and their son, Brett, had graduated from Belmont University in 2013. In 2014, after twenty months with InVentiv, Scott left to start his own company. "I told Ruth, if I do this and fail, I can move on and feel good that I attempted it. If I don't at least try, I will be very disappointed. I'll never know what could have happened. I have to do this."

"I was changing," Ruth says, "but not as fast as Scott."

Never was the tension more palpable than when they sat in a small room at a title company in Wheaton, Illinois, getting ready to put up a condo they owned as collateral for the startup. "Ruth did not want to be there," Scott says, "but she went ahead and signed. The condo was worth $300,000. If the venture succeeded, we'd keep it, and everything would be good. If my dream didn't materialize, we'd be out $300k.

We put other monies into the project as well, but that was a big day."

According to business leader and former presidential candidate Herman Cain, "Everyone has a built-in 'risk index' that's somewhere between 0 and 1.0. . . . If your risk index is 0, you're afraid to get out of bed in the morning for fear there might not be a floor there. But if your risk index is 1.0, you'll jump out of an airplane without a parachute, knowing you're going to find one before you hit the ground! There aren't too many people with a risk index of 1.0, but good leaders need risk indexes that are 'north of 0.5.'"[45]

Scott had a risk index north of 0.5. He took the plunge and asked others to follow, starting with Ruth. Bruce Duncan and his wife, Judy, jumped right on their heels. They soon attracted other skilled and committed accomplices.

4
Accomplices

The main ingredient of stardom is the rest of the team.
—John Wooden

Scott and Bruce came up with $500,000 of their own money to launch OWP Pharmaceuticals, with Scott providing the larger share. But the most valuable asset they brought to the enterprise was experience. Each had about three decades' worth in their respective fields. At their first lunch, Bruce had told Scott that his becoming an expert in pharmaceuticals wasn't an accident. He had been prepared for the second half of his life and his higher calling. The same could be said for Bruce.

Three Careers

In describing himself, Bruce Duncan says, "I'm your typical accountant. If you're familiar with the nine different personality types of the Enneagram, I'm a classic 5. Fives are known as Investigators because we want to understand why things are the way they are. We are content-focused and analytical, with a drive to test the truth of most assumptions for ourselves."

Bruce was born in Evanston, Illinois, in 1954. His family moved around Illinois before settling in Wheaton when he started seventh grade. He attended Wheaton schools through high school, went to Wheaton College, and graduated with a degree in economics. Then on to Case Western Reserve University School of Law in Cleveland, where he got interested in taxation, mergers, and acquisitions. One of the Big Eight public accounting firms had its national headquarters in Cleveland, and Bruce landed an internship with them. He earned his law degree in 1979 while working in public accounting.

He moved back to the Chicago area in June and went to work for Arthur Andersen in August. He stayed for ten years. During that time he passed the CPA exam. He met Judy Mathis at church in 1982 and married her in 1985. Between 1987 and 1996 they had four children: Elizabeth, Sara, Hannah, and Andrew.

In time, Bruce got assigned to be the tax manager for ServiceMaster, then a billion-dollar business headquartered in nearby Downers Grove. One day he happened to run into the CEO, Bill Pollard. "I've known Bill almost all my life," Bruce says. "He was my Sunday school teacher in seventh grade and had been a mentor to me. He was very glad to see me."

Bruce worked on the ServiceMaster account from 1984 until they hired him away from Arthur Andersen to run their tax department in January 1990. Overall revenues were an impressive $1.8 billion, but future growth was hindered by the company being a limited partnership. Over the next several years, Bruce led a corporate restructuring that eliminated the barriers to investment. By the time he left in 2000, overall revenues had doubled.

"I didn't move on because I was unhappy," Bruce clarifies. "I thoroughly enjoyed being at ServiceMaster. But years earlier, after I sat for my bar exam, I was walking in downtown Chicago and I sensed the Holy Spirit talking to me: '*You're going to spend half your career in secular work and then you're going into the ministry.*' That was the first time I had a sense of God speaking directly to me. It made a deep and lasting impression. Ever since then I'd been targeting age forty-five as the point I would transition into some sort of full-time ministry. I even told Bill Pollard this when he recruited me. I said I had ten more years before leaving, and he replied, 'I'll take you for ten years.'"

Bruce was twenty years into his career and forty-five years old at the beginning of the new millennium. True to his calling, he left a lucrative position at ServiceMaster paying in excess of $200,000 and moved his family to Columbus, Ohio. There he and Judy attended the Vineyard Leadership Institute to become church planters. The switch wasn't totally out of the blue. In the early 1990s the Duncans had helped plant a church. Three couples started in their living room what would grow to become Trinity Vineyard in Saint Charles, Illinois.

The Duncans spent two years in Columbus before moving to the northern suburbs of Philadelphia. But after four years of diligently trying to start a church, Bruce realized it wasn't going to work. He was a much better accountant than pastor. He began looking to reenter the secular workforce. A friend of his was the general counsel for a startup capital management company in Wheaton called PowerShares. They were looking for a CFO, and Bruce landed the job.

During his five years there, PowerShares grew to more than $50 billion in assets under management.

This success led to PowerShares being bought by a larger firm, and Bruce's tenure came to an end in 2011. He kept up his private tax business and also became business manager for Glen Ellyn Bible Church for the next eighteen months. During this period he met Scott and began putting time into what would become OWP. This "third career" would blend Bruce's considerable business expertise with his deep passion to serve God by serving people.

Third Man

Neither Scott nor Bruce had experience running a nonprofit foundation. Fortunately, Bruce knew someone who did. Paul Regan had his own thirty years of on-the-job training. In his case, in nonprofit leadership, with a majority of that time in philanthropy and international relief. He had an EdD in nonprofit leadership and had served as CFO, COO, and CEO of various organizations. "I refer to Paul as a Renaissance man," Bruce says. "Anything you need done, Paul can do it. We reached out to him very early on."

Paul would look at home on any college faculty. Six feet tall, medium build, bespectacled, and balding, he's a reserved New Englander without the accent. He's an avid reader of books and an astute reader of people. As the past president of the Christian Association for Psychological Studies (CAPS), the oldest and largest association of Christian behavioral scientists in the US, Paul had connections with psychologists and psychiatrists that he could draw on in his work.

Paul and his wife, Trudy, had been one of the couples to help start the church that met in the Duncans' home. Paul had also served with Bruce on a nonprofit board in the 1990s. When Bruce and Scott asked him to lend his experience and expertise to the foundation side of their social enterprise, he jumped at the chance.

Born in Connecticut in 1959, Paul was raised in Dracut, Massachusetts, where his dad was a teacher and later an assistant superintendent in the public school system. His mother was also a teacher. She later became a town librarian. Education was important to the Regans. Paul grew up to pursue his at the nearby University of Lowell (now the University of Massachusetts at Lowell). He graduated with a bachelor's degree in psychology, went on to earn his master's degree in counseling at Liberty University, then returned to the University of Massachusetts at Lowell to get his doctorate in organizational leadership, with a specialty in nonprofit administration.

During his college years, Paul met and later married Trudy Lenes. Between 1986 and 1989 they had three children: Luke, Carolyn, and Marcus. While getting his degree, Paul worked as assistant director of the Area Health Education Center (AHEC) hosted at the university. Funding for the program dried up in 1991, and Paul went job hunting. He wound up at Interest Ministries in Wheaton, Illinois. This faith-based nonprofit served churches in the US and Canada. Almost three years later, a reorganization erased Paul's position. In March 1994 he became the president of Stewards Ministries, a private funding organization with an annual grant budget of $3 million. Bruce Duncan was on the Stewards' board.

Paul ran Stewards for five years before being recruited by a nonprofit called International Teams (IT). IT was a relief organization with more than 325 personnel working in sixty-five countries. Paul served as executive VP and COO during a five-year stint. He left in 2004 and did consulting for a few years. Then in 2007, IT asked him to return during a time of transition. For the next four years he functioned as executive VP, COO, and CFO. Here Paul got to know and work closely with Stephen Fraser, the chairman of IT's board. Stephen would one day play a key role in OWP's survival.

"I returned to consulting after leaving IT the second time," Paul recounts. "I would meet with Bruce occasionally, and in early 2014 we had lunch. He told me about Scott Boyer and the ideas they were discussing. Bruce asked me to a meeting with key people to get feedback. A few deep-pockets people were there. My pockets had holes in them, but I went to learn more about their plans."

Shortly afterward, Paul was invited to become part of the initial team. No one got paid, nor would they for quite a while. Paul eagerly signed on anyway. "For how I'm wired, this was the opportunity of a lifetime," he says. "I've always been more motivated by humanitarian goals than money. There's no better feeling than knowing I'm helping people in need. Part of this stems from the values instilled in me as a child. And part of it is due to a life goal adopted in early adulthood—that I would always strive to pursue peace, promote justice, and respect the dignity of every human being. That goal is still my northern star and my benchmark for personal success."

For the first year or so, Paul worked both sides of the fence. For OWP, he handled state licensing to sell medications and sent samples to physicians. For ROW, he got the foundation organized and incorporated in Illinois in July 2014. A board was put together composed of Scott, Ruth, Bruce, and Mark Petersen. Paul was appointed president. He guided ROW through the 501(c)(3) approval process, which was granted in February 2015.

"I always felt OWP/ROW would work," Paul muses. "I

just didn't know when. The growth curve was flat at first because there's so much to getting a product to market in pharmaceuticals. We were working full-time but not making any money. Trudy and I spent down our savings. Every six months or so we'd think, *We can't do this anymore.* Then something encouraging would happen and we'd press on. Six months later, it was the same story. *We can't do this.* But somehow we did."

"The first three years will be rough," management guru Peter Drucker warns potential entrepreneurs. "It's not the money that's the crucial resource; it's that ability to survive those first years of hopeful, promising leads that lead nowhere. If you have the emotional fortitude to last three years, you'll succeed."[46]

Pharma Friends

Scott met Bruce at church. It was here he met another key player for OWP, Mark Petersen. Mark had an executive MBA in pharmaceutical marketing and more than twenty years of sales and management experience. At the time he was the director of communication and coordination for Astellas Pharma.

Scott, Bruce, and Mark attended the 2013 Global Leadership Summit at Willow Creek Church. "Scott came out of one session with a very determined look on his face," Mark remembers. "He had this vision of giving back he wanted to tell me about. We met later, and he shared his idea. 'I just need the guts to do it,' he told me."

Scott kept talking to Mark as he developed OWP. Part of Mark's job at Astellas involved calling on neurologists, and he agreed to put together a focus group of them in Rockford, Illinois. On weekends he spent time at Scott's, honing questions for the group. At one point Scott told Mark he would offer him a job someday. "I thought he was a long way from a viable business," Mark recalls. "But I stayed involved and helped in whatever ways I could."

That commitment eventually led to Mark setting up OWP's sales efforts. In the spring of 2016, Scott put him on as regional business director to manage five outside sales reps called NAMs, neurology account managers. Then, in the fall, Mark had to let them go when OWP almost flatlined. His own position evaporated, and Mark, newly married, wrestled with what to do. "My wife, Therese, and I talked about me looking for another job, but nothing came along. I truly believe God kept any great opportunities from materializing. I'm glad we rode it out, but it was hard."

Mark continued to put in time at OWP sans salary. When the company resurrected around its second drug, he rebuilt a more professional sales team. "Now we could afford reps with a lot of pharma experience. Many of the pros we attracted hated Big Pharma but still loved calling on physicians. They also loved our mission and what we were doing because it had a higher meaning. In January 2018 we hired ten more reps and really kicked things off. That's also when I started getting paid again. Like Scott, Bruce, Paul, and the others, I'd been putting in a lot of volunteer time and looking elsewhere to earn income."

Mark's motivation for putting up with the sacrifices and strain were similar to Scott's. "I had worked for a pharma company with great products that really made a difference in people's lives," Mark says. "I loved pharmaceuticals. It's a great match for my gifts and passion. But I often had to give myself a pep talk about the pricing. It just got to be too much. Now, with OWP, I can do what I love, getting essential products to people who need them at a fair cost. And in addition, through the ROW Foundation I can leave a lasting legacy. That's a great feeling."

Another pharma veteran Scott brought into the equation was an old friend from Kansas City named Paul Sudhakar. Dr. Sudhakar had more than thirty years of experience (there's that number again) in the pharmaceutical field. He had his own company, PTS Consulting, that served as the US agent for numerous pharmaceutical firms around the world. Its specialty was helping them prepare for FDA review on drug and biologic manufacturing. Paul resonated with the vision and mission of OWP, and he eagerly helped as a confidant and consultant. Through his connections in the generics market, OWP would find a company to manufacture its first drug.

Next-Gen Buy-In

Two early OWP hires had known about the company from the days it was just a twinkle in their fathers' eyes. "Even before I started working here," Brett Boyer says, "I had a lot of interaction with my dad and other members of the founding group. I would occasionally attend their meetings. Dad had dreamed of doing this since I was in middle school. He wanted to do something good with pharmaceuticals because that's his background. But it took a while for the timing to be right for him and for the family.

"I joined OWP in April 2016 as a sales rep. Then in early August, I switched to inside sales and operations. My role was intentionally vague so I could pivot toward whatever was needed most. I kept plenty busy until everything shut down due to a delay with the FDA and a financial crisis with one of our investors. Despite this, we kept working to get our products approved. Once that happened, and some other roadblocks were cleared, we became profitable."

Brett's previous job had been with Volkswagen, the world's fourth-largest employer at the time. "I was just a number to them," he recalls. "Then I came to OWP, where I'm one of a handful of people, but everyone is making a difference. We're doing something extraordinary through ROW, which is one reason I love working here."

The other family member to join OWP was Hannah Duncan. "I remember Dad mentioning this guy he'd met at church. They talked about a concept they called Social Enterprise 2.0. It sounded awesome, but I never envisioned I would actually be a part of it. At the time I did very competitive sales and consulting. Then I transitioned to running the training department of an IT company. But my dad kept planting seeds by saying things like, 'This is going to take off. We're going to need salespeople.' And I would think, *Yeah, right.*"

In the fall of 2015, Bruce told Hannah about OWP developing a sales department. She interviewed with Scott and Mark around Thanksgiving. When they offered her a job, she gave her two weeks' notice and transitioned to OWP. "I've always liked business," Hannah says. "But I also wanted to impact the world in a positive way. I had majored in business management and international business and had done some stuff with microenterprises in Vietnam and the Dominican Republic."

Hannah started as an outside sales rep but was soon laid off with all the other OWP employees during the shutdown of 2016. "I looked for another job, but I knew Scott and my dad were working hard to keep OWP alive. They asked me to be the inside sales manager without pay until things took off. I readily agreed because I cared about the mission."

Those who came to OWP despite the initial lower pay,

and who stuck around when there was no pay, shared a belief in the mission. *"You cannot 'install' new core values or purpose into people,"* say organizational experts Jim Collins and Jerry Porras in *Built to Last*. *"Core values and purpose are not something people 'buy in' to.* People must already have a predisposition to holding them. Executives often ask, 'How do we get people to share our core ideology?' You don't. You can't! Instead, the task is to find people who already have a predisposition to share your core values and purpose, attract and retain these people."[47]

"I love being here because every single day I'm able to use my skills and talents to help people in places like Venezuela and Armenia and Haiti and rural Illinois through the ROW Foundation," Hannah says. "The only reason OWP exists is to be the financial engine for ROW. The updates and photos from different projects are pinned up all over the office and emailed to our team. I know I'm biased because my dad's a part of it, but I feel blessed to work for such respectable men who have a passion for changing lives. In contrast to the whole Me Too movement, I feel empowered and equal and excited about the opportunities ahead."

From the Center Out

Bruce had a rented office in West Chicago, not far from where he and Scott lived. There a handful of people sat around a plastic folding table and worked on bringing OWP/ROW to life. At this early stage, these Siamese twins had not been separated. Every few minutes conversation would halt as a train rumbled past only yards away.

The agenda for one of the earliest meetings, December 29, 2014, included Illinois registration requirements, the name change from Wheaton Pharmaceuticals to OWP Pharmaceuticals, trademark issues, and a crowdfunding campaign to help launch ROW. Bruce gave an update on the search for investors. "We wanted an organizational structure that would allow both the business and foundation to blossom," Paul recalls. "We focused very intentionally on that."

As noted by Collins, "Business leaders of all persuasions and temperaments can legitimately use their companies to stimulate social change. . . . Keep in mind that social consciousness should not—indeed must not—obscure the importance of disciplined management and sound business practices. . . . To do social good you must first and foremost perform well."[48]

Performing well depends on the performers. OWP/ROW could be pictured as a series of concentric circles. The competency and credibility of people in each circle give confidence to those in the next circle out. At the epicenter is Scott, with Bruce and Paul joining him in the innermost circle. The next circle includes Mark Petersen, Paul Sudhakar, and a few others who would help create the infrastructure for the business and foundation. The third ring includes the investors who supplied the needed capital.

The fourth circle would be composed of physicians and patients in the US who would benefit physically and financially from OWP medications. The outermost circle, the one with the largest circumference, would be filled with people whose lives could be improved by ROW projects. As OWP profits flowed into ROW, this circle would expand.

But could this group of innovators pull it off?

Fred's Mission
Kiserem Epilepsy Foundation

Kenyan Fred Kiserem was working in Iraq when his seizures began. After a seizure-related injury required surgery, Fred began to take epilepsy seriously. When he returned home, he experienced the stigma that people with epilepsy face in Kenya. Many people close to him rejected him after learning about his diagnosis. Deciding to work for change in the perceptions of his community and to empower people with epilepsy in his area, Fred founded the Kiserem Epilepsy Foundation in 2017.

Today the Kiserem Epilepsy Foundation runs awareness campaigns, distributes basic necessities, and offers vocational training to provide a way out of poverty for people with epilepsy. More than one-third of Kenyans live on less than two dollars (USD) per day, and only 20 percent of people with epilepsy take antiseizure medication.

Fred explains, "We envisioned a program to help spread awareness about epilepsy through education and to empower those suffering from the disease by assisting them with medication, care, and a means to financial independence."

ROW Foundation makes ongoing treatment grants to the foundation in the form of Roweepra (levetiracetam), made possible by generous donations from OWP Pharmaceuticals. This reliable supply of medication frees up their limited financial resources for other pressing needs.

5
Drugs of Choice

Innovation requires having at least three things:
a great idea, the engineering talent to execute it,
and the business savvy to turn it into a successful product.
—Walter Isaacson

What motivated Scott to make wholesale changes in his life to launch OWP Pharmaceuticals and the ROW Foundation? "I was, and still am, disturbed by a world in which those who have access to life-saving medications withhold them from those in need simply because they don't have money," he says. "I wanted to fight this medical and pharmaceutical injustice by making effective treatments available to all people at all times in all places. And I saw that such efforts needed to harness the financial muscle of business. Without the business 'flywheel,' we won't be able to address social injustices globally."

But where to start? Which medications for what conditions had the best chance of success? Whatever products he intended to sell had to be commercially profitable. He started to do research while working at

InVentiv and noticed what happened when a drug came off-patent. Sales dropped significantly because of competition from generics. But the decline was not as precipitous with antiepileptic, or antiseizure, drugs.

Scott wondered why these antiseizure drugs didn't follow the pattern. More research brought his attention to what's known as the "narrow therapeutic window." A drug's therapeutic window is the dosage range that provides efficacy without unacceptable side effects or toxicity. A drug with a narrow therapeutic index (NTI) has a narrow safety window that requires tighter manufacturing standards.

The need for consistency is paramount with drugs that affect brain chemistry. Epilepsy patients are reluctant to switch to a less expensive generic for fear of variations from batch to batch. Scott realized that a high-quality branded generic could bridge the gap, and he settled on antiseizure drugs as the initial product line for his new company. "Our first drug was critical. We had to choose one that would do well in the market and be accepted by physicians and patients. It also had to be beneficial for the foundation side of our model. It should be something that could help people in under-resourced parts of the world."

Scott determined from the outset he wouldn't spend the number of years or millions of dollars it would take to develop a new drug. Nor would he focus on a broad range of diseases. The target would be epilepsy and (later) associated psychiatric disorders. The bullets would be generic antiseizure drugs. He soon settled on a promising one called levetiracetam. It has some special properties that make it very effective. Unlike other antiseizure drugs, it's water-soluble, which allows for rapid and complete absorption. It's not metabolized by the liver, as are most other drugs of this type. And it mixes well with other drugs.

The leading branded form of levetiracetam is Keppra,

made by UCB. It went off-patent in 2009. Scott's early market feedback suggested neurologists would be attracted to a high-quality generic antiseizure drug that would be more affordable than Keppra. Keppra had dropped from sales of $710 million in 2006 to $265 million in 2012 as a result of being off-patent. But a quarter of a billion dollars is still a tidy sum. Scott knew such long-term profitability was rare.

Branded Generics

Most people assume that a generic is a generic is a generic. But this isn't always the case. The API—active pharmaceutical ingredient—is the same as the patented medication, but the FDA allows for a "bioequivalence range" that usually amounts to 3.5 percent according to numerous studies. This variation doesn't matter with an antibiotic used occasionally, but it can be significant with an antiseizure drug taken daily for years, or an entire lifetime.

Take a 500 mg tablet, for example. One generic manufacturer's machine might put out pills with 498 mg or 502 mg of the active ingredient. A different manufacturer with different machines could have similar variations. The allowed API range within generics can be as much as 480 mg to 520 mg. Such inconsistencies are what concern physicians and epilepsy patients.

OWP's answer is an oxymoron, a "branded generic." Here's how the labels work:

- ◆ The *brand name* of a drug is the name given by the pharmaceutical company that originally developed it. It is reserved exclusively for the developer.
- ◆ The *generic name* is the name of the active ingredient. It is manufactured with its own generic license and marketed after the exclusive rights of the developer expire. Many generic medicines are marketed using only the generic name.

- A *branded generic name* is the name given to a drug that is bioequivalent to the original but is marketed under another company's brand name, not the generic name.

"When asking for a generic at the pharmacy," Scott explains, "you don't know which manufacturer you'll get. Or how much variance there might be from your previous prescription. But if you ask for a branded generic, which you can do by having your doctor write 'Dispense as Written' on your prescription, you get the same product from the same company every time. Our value proposition is that patients will get the same drug from the same manufacturer with the same active ingredient as the patented med at a much lower price. Patients can have the peace of mind that comes with a brand-name drug at the cost savings of a generic."

The other value proposition Scott hoped people would buy into was that by choosing OWP products they would be helping others with epilepsy around the world through the ROW Foundation. OWP's sales reps would emphasize this message to physicians, and the company would promote it to the public through social media.

During 2014, OWP held focus groups with neurologists in different cities. Scott and Mark laid out their value propositions and asked for feedback. Most of it was positive. If doctors knew patients would always get pills from the same source, they would definitely prescribe a branded generic.

But getting the generics made would be a challenge. The generic marketplace is hard to enter and even harder to survive in. Low profit margins, shortages of active ingredients, or manufacturing delays regularly thin out the competition. Not to mention the aggressive countermeasures of Big Pharma. In a 2017 *Washington Post* article, Carolyn Johnson noted:

Drug companies use the legal system to try to discourage or delay generic competitors. They file "citizen petitions" with the FDA to raise questions about competitors' products. They limit the distribution of their drugs so that other companies can't obtain enough of the product to prove to regulators that their version is equivalent. They merge with competitors. Some take advantage of well-meaning policy incentives, finding old drugs that had never gone through the approval process, collecting the data to have them approved—and then raising the price.[49]

Despite these headwinds, there were at least seventeen companies making the one generic antiseizure drug Scott was interested in—levetiracetam. A necessary prerequisite to joining them would be getting approval on an abbreviated new drug application or contracting with a company that already had one.

Roweepra and Subvenite

Since 1938, new drugs need a new drug application (NDA) approved by the FDA. The Food, Drug, and Cosmetic Act of 1984 created an abbreviated process for generic drug approval, called an abbreviated new drug application (ANDA). What makes it abbreviated is that the manufacturer doesn't have to supply its own clinical test data. The ANDA relies on the data in the original NDA. Even so, it can still take two years or longer to get an ANDA.

This was time Scott didn't want to waste. He went looking for a company that already had an ANDA for levetiracetam. He turned to Paul Sudhaker, aka Kansas City Paul, for assistance. Paul found such a firm and brokered a deal for them to serve as a contract manufacturer. The company would be the exclusive US manufacturer of a branded generic levetiracetam for OWP. "This gave us a lot of creditability," Scott says. "We were now a legitimate pharmaceutical company with FDA credentials and a new drug headed for the marketplace."

Many obstacles still existed, name approval by the FDA being chief among them. It took several months to get "Roweepra" approved. Then OWP had to wait for the drug to be manufactured, a process that began in March 2016. There would be three dosages: 500, 750, and 1000 mg. OWP had to pay for the initial batches of about a million pills each. For some unclear reason the FDA approved the 500 mg pills, but not the other dosages.

The Roweepra 500s arrived in late May, but the FDA didn't approve the other doses until five months later. And it would be another six months for those pills to be manufactured and shipped to OWP. "If Roweepra had been our only product," Bruce says, "we would have gone under by then."

It wasn't.

Number two on Scott's initial list of medications was lamotrigine, the second most popular generic antiseizure drug volume-wise in the US. The patented version is made by Glaxo-Smith-Kline (GSK) under the brand name Lamictal. The first generic version was approved in 2009. Today there are at least fifteen manufacturers of lamotrigine products. OWP's branded generic of lamotrigine is called Subvenite.

GSK makes a Lamictal five-week starter kit that physicians love to prescribe to get patients established on the medication. When Lamictal went off-patent, it stopped promoting the kits, although it still makes them. Most in the medical community thought the kits had disappeared. "Neurologists told us the GSK kits had gone away," Mark

Petersen says. "They really wanted them back, and Scott picked up on this. He found a manufacturer with an ANDA for lamotrigine to develop the kit. We began asking a lot of questions and working to make the kit better. We took samples to some doctors, got their feedback, and kept refining it. And when we came out with our own kit, that was a pivotal time for us. We have the only generic version of the kit on the market."

Lamictal is also prescribed to treat bipolar disorder. This opened the door to the psychiatry market. It quickly became obvious that psychiatrists were easier to call on and more receptive than neurologists. This shift in product led to an expansion of philosophy. OWP amended its mission statement to read, "Our strategic focus is to support psychiatrists, neurologists and patients in the US with beneficial products, and to use a large portion of the profits to provide resources for those living with associated psychiatric and neurological disorders in under-resourced areas around the world."[50]

Bipolar disorder is often "comorbid" with epilepsy. "Comorbidity" is the presence of diseases or disorders co-occurring with a primary disease. Dr. David Ficker of the University of Cincinnati Neuroscience Institute points out that "co-morbid mood disorders are very common in people with epilepsy, with both anxiety and depression being highly prevalent. Depression and/or anxiety can be seen in 20 to 50% of people with epilepsy depending on the population studied."[51] Depression is a primary risk factor for suicide. The rate of suicide among epilepsy patients is about twenty-five times greater than in the general population.

"The vision stays constant, but the path forward can vary with the terrain," Scott says. "In order to change the world you have to be profitable. You can't just wish for something to happen; you have to make it happen. We learned from Roweepra that our products need to have a better profit potential. Products that are multi-sourced are low margin, whereas a single-sourced item, like the starter kit, has a very nice margin, greater profitability, and long-term sustainability."

Failing Forward

If a company creates a quality product that consumers need and offers it at a lower price than its competitors, that company should succeed. But such businesses rarely do, and for a myriad of reasons. Not the least of which are the gatekeepers on the road between company and customer and the trolls under the bridge.

The trolls for OWP included the bureaucrats at the FDA and state licensing agencies. More problematic were the gatekeepers. In the pharmaceutical industry they are the all-powerful wholesalers and PBMs.

Wholesalers have a stranglehold on retail outlets that only grows tighter as retail chains continue to shift away from self-warehousing in favor of direct-store deliveries. As a thirty-year veteran of Big Pharma, Scott was well acquainted with wholesalers. "It's not difficult to get a manufacturer for your product," he maintains. "The issue is getting into the marketplace and making a profit. AmerisourceBergen, Cardinal Health, and McKesson control all the retail outlets. Going head-to-head with them is impossible. We ship to them and they distribute our product, but we can't compete with their preferred generics."

Scott explains the power of preferred generics: "Roweepra has to be specified by the physician by writing DAW (Dispense as Written) on the prescription. But pharmacists sometimes ignore the DAW or tell the patient they can't find Roweepra, even though they could, and fill it with a generic. They are told to fill everything with the 'preferred generic' of the wholesaler. Independents do a better job of filling DAWs. If I send ten patients to Walgreens, five will get my product. If I send them to independents, all ten will get my product. In retrospect, I did not want to battle with Walgreens over an approach I should have known not to fight. It was a bad decision that we had to work through.

"You have to find some exclusivity to compete in this market," Scott adds. "We didn't have that with Roweepra. There was nothing unique about it. We didn't have a 'big hook.' We did with Subvenite, though, and that made all the difference. The maintenance dosages of lamotrigine are made by several manufacturers, but Subvenite is the only generic version of the starter kit. And because it's a branded generic, it's easy for doctors to find and write."

Feedback from physicians informed and confirmed OWP's strategy. "When we called on doctors," Scott recalls, "they told us they loved the starter kits. So, we started doing research on them. We put the brakes on Roweepra and stepped on the gas with the kits. We launched them in October 2017, and we've been profitable ever since. We had to do generic starter kits until our Subvenite kits came out in July 2018. It took that long to get name approval and handle other logistical issues. The kits come in three doses, and there are four maintenance doses of Subvenite patients go on afterward. The maintenance dose is low margin, but we make some money on that as well. The combination is a good financial engine for us."

OWP's monopoly on a branded generic starter kit is unlikely to be challenged. Generic companies are into high volume to get the cost per pill down as low as possible. That's how they make money in a market where the margins are so small. The starter kits don't fit their model. They're low volume. They're complicated. They take time to assemble.

"Subvenite is our cash cow," Scott declares, "but we will always make Roweepra. Not because it will be very profitable but because it's the best overall drug for epilepsy in the world. It's very safe; anyone can take it."

In the Pipeline

The OWP development pipeline currently has five oral suspension drugs widely used in neuroscience for conditions such as depression, schizophrenia, bipolar disorder, and attention deficit hyperactivity disorder (ADHD). OWP has filed patents for the first-ever oral liquid formulations of lamotrigine, topiramate, atomoxetine hydrochloride, quetiapine fumarate, and duloxetine hydrochloride.

A suspension is where the medicine is mixed with a liquid in which it cannot dissolve. A suspension can prolong the action of a drug by preventing rapid degradation. It can mask the unpleasant taste of certain medications. Suspensions are also prescribed for patients who have difficulty swallowing tablets and for some children.

The advantage of a suspension is the manufacturer doesn't have to do clinical trials because they're just putting an existing medication in a new delivery mechanism. But the process still takes about eighteen to twenty-four months to get approval. "Once we get approved on a lamotrigine suspension," Scott says, "we would have exclusivity for at least five years. Exclusivity translates into high profitability, but not enough to attract the major players. A suspension might be only 2 percent of the market. That's chicken feed to them. Our goal is to have several products in small niches that add up. If we can launch a few meds making $15 to $25 million each, in a few years we'll be a $100 million company."

Most of the profit will go to the ROW Foundation and will be used to help people suffering from one of the world's oldest diseases.

6
Treatable Disease

Epilepsy is a disease in the shadows.
—Lynda Resnick

Epilepsy is among humanity's oldest known diseases, with cases documented back as far as 4000 BCE. It's a chronic, noncontagious disorder of the brain affecting people of all ages. It's not terminal, but people with epilepsy have a risk of premature death that's up to three times higher than for the general population.

The World Health Organization (WHO) estimates that around 50 million people worldwide have epilepsy, and with more than 5 million new cases every year, it is one of the most common chronic neurological conditions. Nearly 80 percent of people with epilepsy live in low- and middle-income countries. At least 75 percent of people with epilepsy in these countries don't get needed treatment. And up to

70 percent of people with epilepsy could live seizure-free if properly diagnosed and treated.[52]

Epilepsy is characterized by recurrent seizures—a transient occurrence of signs and/or symptoms due to abnormal, excessive, or synchronous neuronal activity in the brain. Seizures can vary from the briefest lapses of attention or muscle jerks to severe and prolonged convulsions. Frequency of seizures can range from less than one per year to several per day.

Temporary symptoms can include loss of consciousness and disturbances of movement, mood, or mental function. Seizures can cause fractures and bruising and lead to psychosocial issues such as anxiety and depression. One seizure does not signal epilepsy; up to 10 percent of people have one seizure in their lifetimes. But two or more seizures can indicate epilepsy, which can be confirmed with testing.

Most commonly, epilepsy is idiopathic, meaning it has no identifiable cause. This type accounts for 60 percent of those with the disease. Epilepsy with a known cause is called *secondary epilepsy*, or *symptomatic epilepsy*. This type can be caused by:

- brain damage from prenatal or perinatal injuries
- congenital abnormalities or genetic conditions with associated brain malformations
- a severe blow to the head
- a stroke that starves the brain of oxygen
- a brain infection, such as meningitis, encephalitis, or neurocysticercosis
- a brain tumor

Global Burden, Personal Shame

Epilepsy accounts for 0.5 percent of the global burden of disease and has significant economic impact in terms of health-care costs, lost work productivity, and premature death. An estimated 2.4 million people are diagnosed with epilepsy each year. In wealthier countries, annual new cases are between 30 and 50 per 100,000 people. In low- and middle-income countries, this figure can be twice as high.[53]

World powers don't agree on much, but on May 26, 2015, a resolution sponsored by China and Russia concerning the global burden of epilepsy was unanimously approved by the World Health Assembly. The resolution called for coordinated action at the country level to address the health, social, and public knowledge implications of the disease. WHO urged member countries to "support the establishment and implementation of strategies for the management of epilepsy, particularly to improve accessibility to and promote affordability of safe, effective and quality assured antiepileptic medicines."[54]

The WHO followed up with another resolution in 2020 at the Seventy-Third World Health Assembly. It called for scaled-up and integrated action on epilepsy and other neurological disorders, stating:

> Neurological disorders are the leading cause of disability and the second leading cause of death. The five largest contributors are stroke, migraine, dementia, meningitis and epilepsy. Much of the neurological disease burden is preventable, provided that broad public health responses in maternal and newborn healthcare, communicable disease control, injury prevention and cardiovascular health, are implemented. Challenges and gaps in providing care and services for people with neurological disorders exist worldwide, and more so in low- and middle-income countries. The intersectoral action

plan on epilepsy and other neurological disorders will address these gaps through integration of prevention, diagnosis, treatment and rehabilitation for neurological disorders within primary healthcare, which is critical to achieving universal health coverage.[55]

When it comes to epilepsy in the US, the Centers for Disease Control (CDC) noted that in 2015, approximately 3 million adults and 470,000 children had active epilepsy. The actual numbers are higher since adults who are institutionalized weren't counted and about 39 percent of adults who experienced seizures in the past year had not seen a neurologist.

Another key factor that may skew the numbers is they were self-reported. There are still stigmas and consequences that keep some people from identifying with the disorder. These include difficulty getting a driver's license, insurance, and other health-care services. It also raises barriers to certain occupations. Then there's the social price to pay. In 2013, 12 percent of US adults said they would avoid a person who has frequent seizures.[56]

Beyond the physical symptoms are the stigmas and stereotypes that have always surrounded epilepsy. Fear, misunderstanding, and discrimination negatively impact the quality of life for people with the disorder and their families. The discrimination and social shame are often more difficult to overcome than the seizures themselves. This can discourage people from seeking diagnosis and treatment so as not to become identified with epilepsy.

Epilepsy is kind of a "second-class" disorder. People who are treated successfully do not want to talk about it. Those who are having seizures do not want to talk about it either. The personal pressure to keep it private is immense.

"People with epilepsy were once considered to be possessed and demonic, and in the 18th and early 19th centuries they were labeled as insane and locked in asylums," says Diane Patternak, a social worker at Hofstra Medical School, in an article by Elizabeth Shimer Bowers on Everydayhealth.com. Bowers and Patternak go on to dispel certain common stereotypes, summarized below:

> Stereotype: "The most prominent stereotype is that epilepsy is a mental illness."
> Truth: "Individuals with epilepsy do not have a mental illness derived from their seizure disorder."
> Stereotype: Epilepsy is associated with neurological disabilities, such as developmental delay.
> Truth: "The majority of people who have seizure disorders do not have neurological disabilities."
> Stereotype: People with epilepsy are violent.
> Truth: "During a seizure, a person may appear frightened, confused, angry, or combative, but violent behaviors are not associated with epilepsy."
> Stereotype: People with epilepsy cannot hold a job.
> Truth: "Although some individuals may have restrictions, many people with epilepsy are able to work successfully."
> Stereotype: Epilepsy is contagious.
> Truth: "Epilepsy is not contagious. In some cases, it results from a medical condition or injury to the brain. In other cases, the cause is unknown."[57]

Even in enlightened America, epilepsy is misunderstood and marginalized. The late Rodney Dangerfield was a comedian who made a fortune not getting any respect.

Epilepsy is the Rodney Dangerfield of diseases. For instance, most people can name a celebrity or sports figure with Parkinson's disease: Michael J. Fox, Billy Graham, and Muhammad Ali. For ALS: Lou Gehrig, Sam Shepard, and Stephen Hawking. For multiple sclerosis: Richard Prior, Ann Romney, and Montel Williams. Epilepsy afflicts more Americans than these three diseases combined. Those who had or currently have the disease include athletes Florence Griffith Joyner, Alan Faneca, Tiki Barber, and Bobby Jones, and celebrities such as Elton John, Prince, Neil Young, Susan Boyle, and Danny Glover.

"There is an ongoing, significant embarrassment level about it," says Dr. Orrin Devinsky, director of the Epilepsy Center at New York University. "The feeling, for a lot of people, is that it does carry a lot worse stigma than a cancer, or an H.I.V. even. At some level, it's society that needs to wake up and realize it's just another neurologic disorder."[58]

Treatable Disease

While epilepsy has been around for thousands of years, effective drug treatment goes back less than two centuries, as noted by Dr. I. E. Leppik:

> The history of effective drug treatment began with the introduction of bromides in 1857 based on later discredited theories of the cause of epilepsy. Phenobarbital (PB) was introduced in 1912 for the treatment of epilepsy because of its sedative properties. In the 1920s, the major effective development was the ketogenic diet. In 1938, the discovery of phenytoin (PHT) by Merritt and Putnam showed that anticonvulsant activity could be achieved without sedation. PHT was the first AED

[antiepileptic drug] introduced for human use after having been tested for safety and efficacy in animal models.⁵⁹

There is no cure for epilepsy, but the disorder responds to treatment in the majority of cases. Studies have shown that between 75 and 80 percent of patients with idiopathic, generalized epilepsy can be successfully treated with antiseizure drugs.⁶⁰

Antiseizure drugs are effective and relatively inexpensive, but mostly unavailable in low- and middle-income countries. According to a WHO study involving forty-six countries, those living with epilepsy in lower-income countries are the least likely to receive effective medications and proper treatment. And they are about five times more likely to die prematurely than their peers in the general population. The study estimated that the epilepsy "treatment gap," or the proportion of people with active epilepsy who were not receiving treatment, was more than 75 percent in low-income countries and more than 50 percent in most middle-income countries, compared to less than 10 percent in many high-income countries.⁶¹

Accurate diagnosis is the first step toward effective treatment. EEG equipment is the most critical piece of hardware in the diagnosing and treatment of epilepsy. (EEG is the acronym for electroencephalography.) An EEG exam involves placing small electrodes on the scalp to measure minute levels of electrical activity in the brain. Skilled physicians are then able to determine if the pattern is typical of epilepsy and, often, to localize the source(s) of seizure activity and decide the best treatment. After diagnosis, EEG exams play an ongoing role in monitoring the disorder and the effectiveness of treatment.

As with antiseizure drugs, access to EEG equipment and the treatment that would follow is beyond the reach of all but a small minority of the world's population.

OWP's Response

Building his company around antiseizure drugs was a smart business decision for Scott. One report estimated the US market for epilepsy drugs—the three best sellers being Vimpat, Lamictal, and Keppra—at $1.3 billion in 2020. The worldwide market could go from $4.6 billion in 2020 to $5.8 billion by 2027.[62]

But Scott was motivated by his heart as well as his head. As he wrote in his blog:

> When I think about what motivated me to make wholesale changes in my life to launch OWP Pharmaceuticals and the ROW Foundation, the word *compassion* comes to mind. Imagine a friend or loved one suffering with epilepsy in the U.S. Now multiply their challenges ten times over and you begin to get a sense of what those with epilepsy in under-resourced areas go through physically, emotionally, and socially. I want to help mitigate their suffering by leveling the field when it comes to treating their disease.

Scott believes heart is more important than business acumen when first dreaming up a business model. "If you don't have the cause or mission figured out from the beginning, you will not fight for the mission with private equity and venture capital. If you don't fight for the mission, it won't have a chance for survival because of 'exit' pressures applied by your funders."

The future can be made much brighter for people with epilepsy through proper diagnosis, treatment, and medication. This is the driving mission of OWP and the ROW Foundation. It is implemented through projects like one with a US neurologist who travels to Haiti, a country where one in ten children is afflicted with seizures. The neurologist writes:

> We saw a 15-year-old boy who had never been treated for seizures he'd been having his entire life. He had not been able to attend school; the teachers were afraid of him. He had no friends, people made fun of him, they wouldn't even touch him. When I looked at his face, I could see how sad and alone he was. I did an EEG and diagnosed primary epilepsy, which is very treatable. I gave him Roweepra and told his mother, "This will help control his seizures and you can put him back in school. This is a disease of his brain he was born with. You cannot catch it. Give him a hug, hold him. There's nothing to be afraid of."

"I can imagine people all over the world who have never seen a doctor," he adds. "If somebody can get to them with portable machines like mine, train local doctors how to diagnose and treat them, and provide an ongoing supply of effective medicines like Roweepra, it would radically improve their lives."

"The global inequity in care of those with epilepsy is heart-wrenching," Scott laments. "The knowledge and medicines already exist to bring hope and a brighter future to millions. Epilepsy is a global problem that deserves a global solution. We aim to be part of that solution."

Mother and Son
Armenian League Against Epilepsy

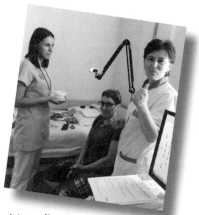

In 2015, ROW granted an EEG machine (used in the diagnosis of epilepsy) to the Armenian League Against Epilepsy (ALAE) for the Arabkir Pediatric Hospital in Yerevan, Armenia. This machine was a major step forward for the hospital being able to effectively diagnose and develop treatment plans for children with epilepsy.

According to Dr. Biayna Sukhudyan, chief of neurology and epilepsy service, "The modern video EEG equipment gave a start to the development of epilepsy surgery in the country. Thanks to our long-lasting partnership [with ROW] many Armenian children with epilepsy have been successfully treated."

One of those children is Benjamin. He had his first seizure one night in January 2012. His mother, Emilia, took him to the hospital and stayed there for three days. During that time he had thirty seizures. "We had to have a good video EEG monitoring unit," recalls Dr. Sukhudyan. "Without that, there was no chance to do surgery. There had been so much work our team had done to get the right equipment. Now, with the help of a video EEG machine, we were able to remove some abnormal pathological brain tissue and Benjamin doesn't have epilepsy anymore. And to know that we're going to change the lives of many other patients through this video EEG machine is priceless."

"I remember my doctor's happy face when she said that we have a new machine; we have a new hope," Emilia says. "I just like the saying, 'We have a new hope.' It's great!"

7
One World. One Standard.

*When it comes to global health,
there is no "them" . . . only "us."*
—Global Health Council

"In November 2017, I was in a meeting in Rwanda with people from a company that did agricultural work," recalls Ken Koskela of Opportunity International. "I saw the terrible consequences of untreated epilepsy. Someone I had arranged to meet did not show up for our appointment. The reason: he had epilepsy and was killed by his community because of it. This encounter left an indelible impression on me. I have epilepsy and know the misunderstanding that still surrounds it."

Rwanda, and the rest of Africa, was relegated to the "ROW column" Scott Boyer used to see while working as a pharmaceutical consultant. R-O-W stands for Rest of World. "Because of geography, politics, and economics, people in ROW countries don't have access to the diagnosis and treatment we take for granted," he says. "My heart breaks for all the human potential that's wasted because these people can't get the care needed to improve their lives—care that's readily available elsewhere."

This concern for ROW countries led to the creation of the ROW Foundation. Its mission is summed up in its tagline: One World. One Standard. It's based on the premise that all people should have the same opportunity for medical treatment, regardless of where they live. In ROW parlance, the phrase "under-resourced areas" is used instead of terms like "First World" and "Third World" or "developed" and "developing" since these terms convey a sense of ranking or superiority.

The "Why"

As related in chapter 4, Scott and Bruce recruited Paul Regan to help set up and run the ROW Foundation, which he was more than happy to do. In his role as spokesman for the organization, Paul sometimes quoted the bestselling author Simon Sinek: "Any person or organization can explain WHAT they do, some can explain HOW they are different or better . . . , but very few can clearly articulate WHY. The WHY is not about money or profit—those are results. The WHY is the thing that inspires us and inspires those around us."[63]

"Our 'why' is very clear," Paul says. "We are laser-focused on improving conditions related to epilepsy and associated psychiatric disorders in under-resourced areas. We provide funding for projects that fulfill our own purpose and that are conducted in coordination with qualified epilepsy-care providers. We measure our success in terms of sustainable impact: how many lives we can help change for the better. Not only will we know when we hit the bull's-eye, but others will know it as well. Our detailed financials are available to the public. The three metrics of intentional action, measurable accomplishment, and organizational transparency provide the stars by which we steer our ship."

Paul's "why" is personal as well as humanitarian. "My sister-in-law, a niece, and a nephew all wrestled with epilepsy. I've seen the life-changing difference the right medications and treatment can make, and I desperately want everyone with epilepsy to have the same chance for a better future."

In working to build ROW's infrastructure, Paul brought Lori Hairrell on board as a part-time program developer. They attended the same church and had known each other for more than fifteen years. "When Paul told me about the ROW Foundation," Lori says with a smile, "he casually mentioned the opportunity to volunteer for an hour or so per week. I agreed to check it out because I knew Paul and had confidence in his abilities. The international aspect also appealed to me. I've done volunteer work with World Relief. I've tutored refugees and helped them adjust to life in the US. I could see ROW would help a lot of people in a big way once it got off the ground. I could also see that with the great needs of the global epilepsy community, a few hours a week wouldn't cut it. But I was hooked. ROW's vision and mission appealed to my sense of justice."

Like everyone involved with ROW, Lori has a deep desire to balance the scales when it comes to medical treatment. "To learn that millions of people around the world live with untreated epilepsy was startling," she admits. "That kind of suffering is so unnecessary. I want to connect people with epilepsy to resources that will enable them to flourish in spite of their condition."

For the first several months of ROW's existence, Paul and Lori focused on building relationships with individuals, professional groups, and associations that could assist ROW in carrying out its mission. Internally, they emphasized getting key systems in place: accounting, communications, social media platforms, and more. They spent time creating a portfolio of written and electronic material to promote the ROW brand and educate the public about global epilepsy.

Paul got involved with ROW in 2014 and Lori in 2015. Neither got a penny from the foundation until January 2017, when both started receiving a part-time salary. The next addition to the team was Ken Koskela, mentioned above. He became aware of ROW in 2016 when a mutual friend introduced him to Scott. Given Ken's MBA in international business and finance, and his more than twenty-five years of experience with international nonprofits, Scott encouraged him to connect with Paul.

"I met Paul on a few occasions and got to know more about OWP and ROW," Ken says. "Prior to that, I had no idea there was a social business with a focus on epilepsy. I have epilepsy and so felt an immediate personal connection to their mission. I had my first seizure at age thirteen while sledding. I woke up surrounded by paramedics and was taken by ambulance to a nearby hospital, where I was diagnosed with epilepsy. Shortly thereafter, I saw a neurologist and began taking medication, which, fortunately for me, has completely controlled my seizures ever since. Because I was so successfully treated, I didn't think about epilepsy very often after that. In 2017 I began a consulting role with the ROW Foundation and learned that the treatment gap in many of the places where I traveled exceeds 90 percent."

A year later, ROW engaged Ken part-time as director of global programs with a view to a full-time position in the future. "Global" is a good descriptor for Ken. For more than twenty years, he'd worked for Opportunity International. He'd traveled to more than ninety countries and visited Africa at least eighty times. He'd helped launch multimillion-dollar initiatives and overseen program design and management around the world.

When Paul was asked to serve as OWP's full-time COO in April 2018, Ken became acting president of ROW. Ken had already determined to make epilepsy a key focus of the remainder of his career and saw this as the perfect opportunity to utilize his skills and experience.

The Programs

ROW secured its IRS designation as a 501(c)(3) private foundation in February 2015. Two months later it chose its first project. ROW would purchase EEG equipment for the Arabkir Pediatric Hospital in Yerevan, the capital of Armenia. The price tag: $24,000. While the original thinking had been for the foundation to provide epilepsy medications not normally available in low- and middle- income countries, Paul had helped broaden the vision to include training professionals and providing equipment to diagnose and treat the disease—hence, an EEG machine.

OWP hadn't made any money yet, so ROW launched an Indiegogo crowdfunding campaign. It raised $6,000, and individuals contributed the rest, including Scott and Ruth. While ROW wouldn't be dependent on such private gifts, they would always be welcome. And because OWP's profits would cover all general and administrative expenses, every dollar given by donors would go directly to help those in need.

On June 26, ROW placed an order with Natus Neurology for a thirty-two-channel video EEG machine to be built and shipped to Armenia. EEG tests help to diagnose epilepsy and to establish the correct treatment. The machine was delivered in July. Dr. Biayna Sukhudyan supervised the grant. She's chief of neuropediatrics at the hospital and vice president of the Armenia national chapter of the International League Against Epilepsy (ILAE). A year later, she reported the hospital had examined about one hundred patients with the equipment, all of them difficult-to-treat cases. By 2020, more than seven hundred children had benefited from this diagnostic technology and ongoing grants of medications not consistently available in Armenia.

This equipment grant would be the first of many. With ILAE's assistance, ROW identified several key locations where EEG equipment would make a crucial difference to under-resourced populations. Since Armenia, ROW has made EEG equipment grants in Sudan, the Republic of Georgia, and India.

Along with helping to provide equipment, ROW is partnering with health-care providers to expand training and educational programs. And since interpreting EEG tests requires specialists who are in short supply in under-resourced countries, ROW has teamed up with TeleEEG, a registered charity in England and Wales. TeleEEG establishes and supports epilepsy clinics in low-income countries. For each clinic, TeleEEG provides an EEG machine and trains local health-care professionals to do EEG tests. TeleEEG then analyzes test results through their team of volunteer neurophysiologists.

"There's no question that telemedicine will have an unbelievable impact in under-resourced areas," Scott says. "Whereas before you had to send people and equipment on planes, now people in these places can get the benefit of neurologists and epileptologists through telemedicine. There are so many doctors who hear about what we're doing and they'll say, 'Oh, I'd love to help, but I can't drop my practice for three weeks and fly over there. But if I can help people by reading EEGs over here, I'm happy to do that.' Technology will allow so many people who have been blessed to live in the US or Canada or the UK to help others around the world. The impact will be phenomenal. The stories are, and will continue to be, incredible!"

Another ROW endeavor involves training and utilizing community health workers (CHWs). One example is ROW's partnership with Boston Children's Hospital. BCH works with children who have epilepsy in Chongwe, Zambia, using CHWs. They are equipped, trained, and mobilized to provide basic care for many common illnesses. While CHWs are usually not typically equipped to support epilepsy care, ROW believes they hold great potential for identifying children in need and connecting them and their caregivers with treatment options.

At the core of ROW's strategy is granting an ongoing supply of antiseizure drugs provided by OWP. "When we enter into a partnership with health-care providers, it's a long-term commitment because epilepsy is a lifetime struggle," Paul says. "We don't want to start people on helpful treatment that can't be sustained."

The first shipment of OWP's Roweepra went to the Arabkir United Children's Charity Foundation for the Arabkir Pediatric Hospital where the EEG equipment had been sent. Since then, ROW has begun supplying meds to hospitals and medical clinics in almost twenty countries, as well as to organizations in the US.

In 2017 ROW gave medication grants with a wholesale value of around $75,000 and financial grants of $8,000. By the fall of 2018 it had made more than thirty grants in more than a dozen countries, with a wholesale value of more than $3.5 million. By 2021 ROW had sponsored dozens of programs in thirty countries, which included granting more than 145,000 patient prescription months of antiseizure medication for people who would otherwise go without. "I foresee a day when we'll be considering 120 proposals a year and granting millions in medication and financial aid," Paul says. "We will be proactive in discovering needs and reactive in responding to needs brought to our attention by reputable organizations."

There's no question ROW has been busy, but has it been effective? One way to measure success is by something called Social Return on Investment (SROI). SROI measures the social, environmental, and economic costs and benefits of an organization, program, or project. An SROI analysis generates a financial ratio comparing "value in" with immediate and long-term "value out." This allows investors or donors to know the economic and social benefit of their involvement.

In the spring of 2017, ROW retained the Social Enterprise Institute (SEI) at Elizabethtown College to conduct an independent SROI analysis. The analysis focused on ROW's Kenya Mobile EEG Project. It considered the SROI for ROW's contribution to the project, as well as the SROI for the larger enterprise of OWP and ROW together. Two ratios were generated:

1. A ratio of $4.95 return to $1.00 investment, representing the SROI for the social enterprise entity of OWP and ROW together
2. A ratio of $57.54 return to $1.00 investment, representing the SROI for ROW's donor dollars paid into the project

In 2018, the ROW Foundation earned the GuideStar Platinum Seal of Transparency, the highest level of recognition offered by the world's largest source of information on nonprofit organizations. This puts them in the top 0.5 percent of profiles in what *Time* magazine calls "the nation's premier nonprofit database."[64]

The Partners

Despite the importance of addressing the epilepsy treatment gap in under-resourced regions, there are surprisingly few global organizations focused on it. What further distinguishes ROW from many other organizations is twofold: First, most others are heavily dependent on donations and grants to fund their operations. Because ROW's operating costs are covered by OWP's profits, all donated funds are directed straight to our programs and partners.

Second, ROW is a funding foundation, not an operating foundation that runs its own programs. It fulfills its mission by supporting well-established organizations that have proven programs. Because of its global reach, ROW is able to add value beyond funding by also sharing lessons learned from one partner to another. ROW isn't interested in reinventing the wheel; it exists to grease the ones that are effectively rolling so as to cover more territory.

In keeping with its belief in the power of teamwork, ROW works in concert with more than fifty partners, including such key international organizations as the International League Against Epilepsy (ILAE) and the International Bureau for Epilepsy (IBE).

Working smarter often means partnering with others by pooling resources and expertise to reach common goals. In a conversation with a past president of the ILAE, Paul mentioned ROW's intent to do a study on the diagnostic equipment and antiseizure drugs available around the world to determine the areas of greatest need. "He told me the ILAE, WHO, and the IBE were jointly working on just such a report," Paul recounts. "It didn't make sense to do our research when these larger organizations had already undertaken this strategic project. Instead, we made a financial gift to their study, which will help us prioritize our projects in the coming years."

Around the world and at home, ROW is cultivating relationships with leading epileptologists, neurologists, and psychiatrists—the latter because, as noted earlier, epilepsy is often comorbid with various psychiatric disorders. "Along with OWP, we've expanded our vision beyond epilepsy," Paul explains. "Many under-resourced countries don't have neurology as a medical specialty. Epilepsy falls under psychiatry in these countries, so working there has meant working with psychiatrists. And Dr. Rossi, a leading epileptologist on our advisory board, informed us that perhaps 30 percent of the time, epilepsy is comorbid with associated psychiatric disorders. Our efforts now take this into account."

Dr. Marvin Rossi is the former co-director of the Multimodality Neuroimaging and Neuroengineering Laboratory at the Rush Epilepsy Center in Chicago. He's only one of the experts who serves on ROW's board of directors or advisory board, and only one of the many professionals who are catching the OWP/ROW vision and bringing their skills and resources to the movement.

Another engaged professional, Keith Morgan, is the founder of Neurotech, LLC, a provider of in-home EEG testing. "I met Scott and Paul, and through them I got connected to a neurologist planning trips to Kenya and Haiti. I've been able to do detailed training sessions via web conferences with the techs he's trained. Teleconferencing is great, but I believe training is best done in person. That's why Neurotech has designated money, equipment, and staff to follow our EEG machines into the field."

ROW isn't interested in credit or control in these relationships. It doesn't have to impress donors or elbow out other organizations for a share of the philanthropic pie. It has no problem playing a supporting role because it doesn't have competitors, only comrades in a common cause: to provide the highest attainable standard of health to everyone struggling with epilepsy and associated psychiatric disorders.

Initially, the more established organizations viewed ROW with caution. "When Paul and I first met with the ILAE," Scott recalls, "their initial response was, 'So what if you can help for a quarter, or a year; can you do it for a lifetime?' Because of what ROW has been able to do since 2015, and our commitment to sustainability, they are now big believers and solid partners."

"ILAE is very interested and supportive in what we're doing," Lori agrees. "They've seen what we've been able to accomplish on a limited budget. We meet with their management committee during the American Epilepsy Society annual meeting. It's a credibility we've earned and intend to keep."

The Challenges

"There's far more to do than we have resources for," Paul readily admits. "That will change as OWP becomes more profitable and ROW receives more revenue or royalties from the company. I believe our model will allow us to become the world's largest funder of projects serving people with epilepsy and associated psychiatric disorders. In today's business world, companies are built to be sold for maximum profit for the founders. What Scott and Bruce did from the outset is make sure this wouldn't happen."

Just as OWP has had to adjust and adapt to changing circumstances and new information, ROW has had to shape-shift to effectively pursue its mission. "ROW is a private foundation," Paul explains. "As a 501(c)(3) private foundation, we can take charitable contributions, but there are some limitations. Private foundations are often associated with a single funding source. As such, they aren't subject to all the same regulations as other charities, and they don't do a lot of fundraising among the general public. Consequently, they don't attract many outside donors, even if they believe in the foundation's mission.

"But there's another type of 501(c)(3) called a public charity," Paul continues. "Public charities have a more advantageous tax status with the IRS, as well as some other benefits. Based on advice from nonprofit attorneys and advisors, we've recently chosen to create a public charity to work alongside our existing private foundation. ROW will be both a private foundation and a public charity. The two will be like conjoined twins. People and entities who want to give to a public charity can give to ROW's public charity. Those who want to fund our work through a private foundation can give to ROW's private foundation. These two options will increase our funding and expand the work we can do around the world."

"We want to get the word out about ROW any way we can," Scott says. "It could be through videos, social media, someday an app that lets people follow what we're doing and even donate with the few clicks. We will lean in to the technology of today to reach donors, medical professionals, and people who could support or use the foundation's help.

"I'm not certain why I began asking questions about the social injustice behind the 'ROW' designation," Scott adds. "Perhaps it was my age, the time in my career, or that Ruth and I were entering the empty nest phase. Whatever the reasons, I felt like I had to do something."

Peter Drucker once said that the mission of nonprofits is changed lives. The mission of the ROW Foundation is to change the lives of millions of people with epilepsy and associated psychiatric disorders who are sitting on the sidelines, hoping to get into the game. New diagnostic equipment and treatment methods don't have to be invented to reach those living beyond the horizon of modern medicine. What's been missing is a means of distribution that's self-supporting and scalable.

Not anymore.

The OWP/ROW model represents a paradigm shift in health care for billions of underserved people in ROW countries and millions more in the US, where prescription costs are often astronomical. It proves there's more than enough margin in pharmaceuticals to provide a healthy profit *and* to help those in need. What they're doing for epilepsy patients can be done for people dealing with cancer, heart disease, diabetes, and a myriad of other disorders.

The World Health Organization's Constitution sees "the highest attainable standard of health as a fundamental right of every human being."[65] Anything less, as Martin Luther King Jr. said, is inhuman.

The people behind OWP and ROW believe this injustice can be remedied. One World. One Standard. is possible if enough good people decide to make it so. But they also know that good intentions, while commendable, are not sufficient to bring about lasting change. For that you need capital.

The old adage is still true: no money, no mission.

8
No Money, No Mission

If you have a conviction that what you want to do is worthy, you may have to sell the idea to others to raise the needed capital.
—John Bradley

"Capital" is the money needed to produce goods and services. Capital for businesses can be raised through debt and equity. Debts must be repaid whereas equity bestows an ownership position that usually comes in the form of stock. If the company prospers, the stock pays dividends. If the company fails, investors lose their investment.

Scott and Bruce began OWP with a half million dollars of their own money. This seed capital lasted about a year. They watered it with long hours of free labor. Their first paid employees were two college interns kept busy calling neurologists and pitching OWP's new drug. When the time came to sign a contract with a manufacturer in Taiwan, they put together a business plan and went looking for investors.

They quickly discovered their hybrid model wherein the

ROW Foundation received a big chunk of company profits didn't interest venture capitalists (VCs). "We tried to get investors who wanted to make money but also wanted to have a positive impact in the world," Scott explains. "If you know VCs, you know this mindset isn't very common. We talked to one VC we thought would be willing to accept a little lower return because of what we intended to do with ROW. He sent back a note saying, 'You should change your name to Robin Hood Pharmaceuticals.' That took me aback. He saw us as taking from the rich and giving to the poor. And he didn't mean it in a positive manner."

Scott and Bruce would have to rely on family, friends, and angel investors to fund their vision, not VCs. Angel investors use their own money to invest in businesses. They have to be accredited, which affirms they have a minimum net worth of $1 million and an annual income of at least $200,000. Venture capitalists can be individuals or firms that use money pooled from investment companies, corporations, or pension funds.

Angels take a higher risk as they put up their own money, whereas VCs invest other people's money. The first group typically invests between $25,000 and $100,000. VCs invest an average of $7 million in a company. They're shooting for a tenfold return within five years, primarily because they expect at least half of the enterprises they back to fail.

Bruce's brother invested, as did some of Scott's siblings. A few of Scott's associates in the pharmaceutical industry wanted in when he told them what he was doing. These early investors had a like-minded desire to address injustice. They could reasonably expect a good financial return on investment, but they mainly wanted to have a positive social impact through people they knew and trusted.

When they approached Bruce's former mentor and

boss, Bill Pollard, he told them their idea wouldn't work. "You have to sell to doctors, and you can't do that under our current system," he said. "Doctors all work for hospitals, and hospitals don't want them talking to pharmaceutical reps. Thanks, but no thanks."

Stocks, Bonds, Units

Because of feedback from high-net-worth individuals, Scott and Bruce decided to change what they offered investors. "Originally we thought of selling stock with a call option," Bruce says. "Then we restructured to what we called an 'investor unit.' It had a bond that paid 6 percent interest over five years and a warrant to buy one-half of 1 percent of OWP common stock for a minimal fee at the end of that time. The bond seemed a better way to ensure investors would get their money back with a little interest. We wanted to sell twenty units at $50,000 each to raise a million dollars. We did this over the next year or so, which kept us going."

Scott and Bruce sold the right to buy approximately 25 percent of OWP stock to investors via the investment units. They kept 75 percent of the stock themselves. They planned to give the majority of this to ROW. "In order to carry out our vision of ROW owning a majority of OWP stock," Bruce explains, "the stock comes with a 'legend.' The term comes from the fact that stock is actually a piece of paper. Just like with a personal check, you can write something on the back that puts some type of restriction on the ability to transfer it. The practice isn't common but it's completely legal. We put a legend on our stock that says the ROW Foundation has a right to buy back up to half of it at fair market value.

"Once ROW bought half of the 25 percent of stock sold to investors, it would be entitled to 12 percent of company profits," Bruce adds. "That, plus the 30 percent of stock donated by Scott and me would increase their dividends to more than 40 percent. Add to this the 10 percent pretax donation OWP gives the foundation annually and ROW would receive half of company profits."

It was an elegant plan, but one that turned out not to work. The IRS doesn't allow a not-for-profit (NFP) to have a controlling interest in a for-profit, so NFPs can't own more than 20 percent of the voting stock. "We also discovered that for federal tax purposes, it's better that ROW does not hold an ownership interest in OWP," Bruce says. "As a private nonoperating foundation, ROW is subject to a certain excise tax and self-dealing rules that would be triggered by a direct ownership interest in OWP."

"The experts looked at Bruce's original structure for OWP and ROW," Paul says, "but they thought there could be a better way to accomplish the same goals with fewer limitations. Bruce wasn't offended or defensive. He shifted his thinking and said, 'I see what you're saying. Now, what if we did it this way?' They listened to Bruce, who really deserves credit for the second plan as well as the first. The end result was an equally effective, but more elegant and powerful plan."

Bruce explains the details: "Our new plan is for OWP to transfer its intellectual property—trademarks, copyrights, product patents, and licenses—into wholly owned, limited liability holding companies. They will license certain rights to OWP in exchange for royalties equal to a percentage of gross sales. These companies will have two members, OWP and ROW. As a member, ROW will receive a percentage of the royalties paid by OWP. The royalty income isn't subject to business income tax or excise holding tax."

The new plan also addresses Scott and Bruce's commitment to protect ROW from OWP being sold out from under it. The governing documents for the holding companies specify that any decision about sale of membership is subject to ROW Foundation's sole veto. This ensures that ROW's financial underwriting is continuous and secure, now and for the future.

Making the Rounds

In October 2017, OWP was invited to the Lion's Den, a Christian version of *Shark Tank* held in Birmingham, Alabama. The event, hosted by the nonprofit Cedarworks, Inc., was created "to inspire, educate, and mobilize professionals to use their time, talents, and other resources for advancing God's Kingdom through business as mission."[66] Each year it highlights four businesses presenting to more than three hundred attendees and a Panel of Lions. These judges are looking for "sharp business minds focused on producing financial, social, environmental, and spiritual results in their chosen endeavors, known as the quadruple bottom-line." The presenters are looking for investors.

The featured businesses are for-profit, marketplace companies with solid foundations and promising futures. Their founders have more in mind than making money, but they take seriously the moneymaking aspect.

OWP was featured, and Scott titled his presentation "Social Enterprise 2.0: The New Frontier of Social Capitalism." His main points were the following:
- ◆ Medicines existed that could improve millions of lives, but they weren't available in much of the world.
- ◆ Big Pharma wasn't going to substantially address these medical and pharmaceutical injustices because there was no profit in doing so.
- ◆ There was a large market for antiseizure drugs in the US that OWP could reach with its branded generics.

It could reasonably expect to capture 6 percent of the market.
- ◆ Profits or royalties from US sales went to the ROW Foundation to fund life-changing projects among the more than 50 million people living with epilepsy in low- and middle-income countries.
- ◆ Evaluation of a recent OWP/ROW project by the Social Enterprise Institute showed a $4.95 SROI for every dollar spent.
- ◆ The OWP/ROW model was not only a philanthropic success; it was scalable and sustainable.

The presentation resulted in OWP getting almost a million dollars in new investments to keep the dream alive. This would cover product development and operations going into 2018.

Capital Concerns

Businesses need money to grow, but there's an inherent risk in depending on investors to fuel that growth. The next chapter goes into more detail about how Scott and Bruce raised the capital it took to go from shaky vision to solid ground. And the price they almost paid for it.

"You have to be very cautious with private equity and venture capital funds," Scott warns from experience. "Even if they're a minority stakeholder, they may have majority rights based on the terms of your agreement. They can force decisions that are in their short-term interest but not in the best long-term interest of the company."

Scott notes another pitfall to avoid: selling too much of your dream. "If you don't think this through when you're starting out, you're going to be in trouble. You go to your angel investors in round one and sell some equity. But then you may need to go to other investors or private equity firms in rounds two and three. Every time you do this, you give away more of the company. Before long, you no longer own a majority interest. Once that happens, it's too late. It's just a matter of time before they take over and sell what you've built. And there goes your plan, your purpose, your calling. I was at the Lion's Den conference one year and heard a Christian VC boast, 'Oh yeah, I've had to fire founders before; that's no big deal. They had good ideas and got things to a certain point, but they couldn't get any farther, so we had to bring another management team to take over.'"

To hold on to the dream, Scott and Ruth had to take some big risks and make some even bigger sacrifices. So did those who joined them. Scott and Bruce worked for nothing for more than three years. So did Paul and Mark and others who got involved early on. "As I look back on all the sacrifices," Scott says, "they were worth it. If we hadn't been willing to stick with it through those tough times, we would never have made it. Back when Roweepra fell off the cliff, we had to fire people. We couldn't cut our own salaries because we weren't being paid. Not until we got our second product out there could we start paying ourselves and the other people somewhat normal salaries. And now we're in a position where we don't have to sell any more equity and can actually start buying some of it back from our initial investors.

"The easy thing is to lean into the investors who can make your life a lot smoother," Scott adds. "But in the end they have so much invested that they can push you around. They want to make money and they can micromanage you. They can even pull you under."

There are other dangers besides contrarian investors that can sink a new venture, as Scott and Bruce would soon find out.

Bety's New Chapter
ASLEK Epilepsy Foundation

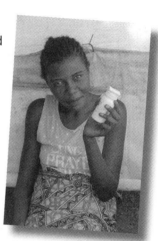

Because poverty and the epilepsy treatment gap go hand in hand, the ROW Foundation was delighted when Dr. Prince Kazadi reached out to us regarding a partnership in the Democratic Republic of the Congo (DRC).

In 2015 Dr. Kazadi organized ASLEK Epilepsy Foundation in Lubumbashi, the DRC's second-largest city. He sees the effects of stigma on people with epilepsy. They are shunned socially, and sometimes endure physical, psychological, or sexual abuse at home or in the community. Poor patients face difficult choices between buying medication, feeding their families, or paying school fees. ASLEK provides support for patients and families, educates the public through schools and community campaigns, and lobbies for better conditions from government.

Eighteen-year-old Bety Mutombo lived with untreated seizures for more than five years. In May, she began treatment with Roweepra given to ASLEK by ROW. Today, Roweepra controls Bety's seizures, enabling her to hold a sales position at a local supermarket. Bety is one of five hundred–plus patients under ASLEK's care. The opportunity to gain financial independence helps patients like Bety begin a new chapter.

Dr. Prince Kazadi stresses how greater availability of antiseizure drugs leads to better seizure control, which increases an individual's employment prospects. ROW medication support gives physicians drug choices they may not be able to access otherwise. ROW also introduced Dr. Kazadi to TeleEEG, our partner specializing in epilepsy diagnosis by telemedicine. ASLEK has already received EEG equipment from them and has begun offering EEG services to clients.

9
Minefield

*Experience is what you get when you
didn't get what you wanted.*
—Randy Pausch

There's a *Far Side* cartoon that shows a caveman tied on top of a large stone wheel perched on the crest of a hill. Another caveman waits below, clipboard in hand. The caption reads, "Early experiments in transportation." In 2015 Scott and Bruce tied themselves to their dream and were ready to roll.

Both men had enough business experience to know they would be rolling through a minefield. A 2019 report by Startup Genome claims that eleven out of twelve business startups fail. Entrepreneurial coach Eric Wagner lists the main reasons for failure, which include lack of a clear value proposition, a breakdown in leadership, and not enough revenue.[67]

OWP had a very clear and distinct value proposition. It

had seasoned leadership with decades of success in their fields. Cash would be their first major challenge. Sweat equity was a major component of the compensation plan.

Mixed Blessing

Because of their Halftime connection, Scott and Bruce were invited to a gathering of high-net-worth individuals at the Ritz-Carlton in Scottsdale, a nice venue for late February. They mingled with about one hundred potential investors for the weekend. OWP was among the four alumni stories highlighted before the group. In preparation, Halftime had interviewed Scott and Ruth. They even sent a film crew to Armenia, where ROW's first grant had provided a $24,000 EEG machine to a pediatric hospital in the capital city of Yerevan.

One attendee who was starting a venture capital fund thought OWP would be a great initial investment. A dialogue ensued that ultimately led to a deal. The VC fund agreed to put $2 million into OWP. As part of the deal, it wanted the operations to be inside an LLC, not a C-Corp, which is what OWP was. The transition would be difficult, but Bruce agreed to do it. All business would be done by the LLC. The fund would invest $2 million in the LLC in exchange for 18 percent of OWP. This was originally 9 percent but was raised to 18 percent when the initial product launch did not materialize as planned.

Unforeseen problems soon arose because of this arrangement, as Bruce explains: "To sell pharmaceuticals you need to be licensed by each state. It had taken us nine months to get all our licenses. I assumed we could just transfer them to the LLC. Wrong. The new business had to get its own licenses. And each business had to have its own address, so we couldn't use the OWP address for the new LLC. Fortunately, my office had two doors. I went to the city of West Chicago and got a second address for the second door. Our operations had now expanded to 931 West Hawthorne and 933 West Hawthorne.

"We were still working through the licensing hassle when time came to close on the deal with the VCs. I told them we didn't have our licenses yet and so couldn't ship any product. They proposed putting $1.2 million into the LLC and withholding the remaining $800,000 until we got our licenses. We agreed to these terms, and their attorneys created a note between the LLC and OWP. This is where I made a huge legal blunder. I didn't look carefully at the note. It turned out to be a demand note, which meant they could call it in at any time. This was August 6. Fast-forward to about September 20. Scott's in Colorado on vacation when he gets a call from the VCs. 'You're missing your numbers. We want all our money back!'"

Bankers have often been accused of being people who would gladly lend you an umbrella—but want it back the minute it begins to rain. The same could be said of VCs.

Several days later, Bruce sat in Scott's kitchen, on a conference call with the VCs. They were calling their note. "They wanted their $1.2 million back now!" Bruce recalls. "This was impossible. We'd spent almost $500,000 already. They said, 'How can you blow that much money in two months?' We thought the world was going to end. They would take us to court and close us down.

"I knew we needed some money to keep going," Bruce continues. "I went to the bank and converted the balance in the OWP account into a cashier's check for $200,000. I took this back to the office and put it in the safe. If the VCs decided to get an injunction and freeze our accounts, we'd at least have some money to operate. In the meantime, I wired them the balance in the LLC, about $700,000. There was a lot of tension. They saw us as robbers and shysters. We saw them as greedy SOBs. It was a bad situation."

"This was this VC group's first major deal," Scott reflects. "They were in more of a panic than us. We weren't giving up. We told them Plan A hadn't worked, so we're going to Plan B. We felt pretty good that Plan B would work."

Within a week of the acrimonious call, Scott and Bruce had lunch with Stephen Fraser. They hadn't seen him since he'd become an angel investor back in January. He quickly discerned something was wrong and pressed for details. "We told him what had happened and the disastrous mess we were in," Bruce says. "The first thing he asked was, 'You didn't send them any money, did you?' I had to admit I had. 'Well, don't send them any more.'"

After lunch, Stephen drove directly to the VC's office and told them they had to work this thing through. He assumed the role of negotiator between the two parties. Discussions went back and forth over the next weeks on ways to restructure the original deal. During that time OWP had to lay off all its staff. Scott had to tell his son, Brett, and Bruce his daughter Hannah that their jobs had disappeared.

Stephen had also invested in the VC fund, which gave him some leverage. He had a stake in both sides and was able to arbitrate a compromise. In the end, the VCs agreed not to call their note. They dropped their demand for an LLC and let OWP stick with its original structure. This made the licensing problem disappear.

The "Pearl of Great Price," as Stephen called it, was that OWP had the right to buy out the fund at any time within the next year. "Even though this was a traumatic time for OWP," he says, "it's not because the VCs were bad guys. They were doing exactly what venture capitalists do, and OWP was doing exactly what startups do. The tension that erupted is fairly typical in such situations."

Daylight Ahead

As part of the deal with the VCs, Scott and Bruce had to put another $100,000 into OWP from their own pockets. If they needed more money, they would have to raise it.

They did, so they went back on the road early in 2017 looking for new investors. Their most receptive leads came from Stephen Fraser's Rolodex. Once again, they offered investor units composed of a bond and a warrant. But since OWP was more established by now, it would cost $50,000 to exercise the warrant. Instead of getting stock just for loaning money, investors had to buy the stock at that price.

Scott and Bruce raised $900,000, and the VC fund put in another $600,000. This $1.5 million enabled them to launch their second product, which promised to be a game-changer. They hired four college interns to call doctors around the country. They logged more than seven thousand positive responses. There was hope on the horizon.

Scott and Bruce then went looking for additional cash to buy out the VC fund. Scott contacted a loan broker named Bob who had coached Brett Boyer's baseball team some years earlier. Bob connected them to Busey Bank. After completing their due diligence, the bank offered OWP a $1.5 million loan. "I'm still amazed we got it," Bruce says. "No one else would help us, but Busey was aggressively trying to get into the Chicago business market."

The loan gave OWP enough to settle up with the VCs. They did so on February 28, 2018. With this burden lifted, OWP could now devote some financial attention to their investors.

One reason the investor units had bonds was so OWP could pay interest on them whether the company was profitable or not. But the VCs had forbidden the company to give anything to other investors until they got all their money back. As soon as that happened, OWP made a six-month interest payment on the outstanding bonds.

To Market, to Market

The cash flow crunch almost derailed the OWP enterprise. Getting its product manufactured and to market in a timely way proved another hurdle. The company manufacturing OWP's first medication, Roweepra, did an initial run of three dosages. The FDA approval the 500 mg pills but not the 750 mg or 1000 mg.

"We wrestled with whether to order the 500s while waiting for the other dosages to be approved," Bruce vividly recalls. "This was our first big-risk decision. Do we try to sell the 500s without the 750s or 1000s? We kicked it around and finally decided that we'd been working for two years and needed to get rolling. We pulled the trigger and ordered the 500s. I had no experience with the FDA, but it seemed obvious that they would approve the other doses of the exact same drug. It was a no-brainer. How long could it take?"

Months, it turned out.

The Roweepra 500s arrived at OWP in late May, but the FDA didn't approve the other doses until October 31. "I remember it was Halloween when we finally heard we could sell the other dosages," Bruce says. "Not having all the doses from the outset caused a major problem with our original launch."

Unexpected FDA delays also created a crisis with OWP's second drug, a version of the generic lamotrigine. The patented drug, Lamictal, came with a five-week starter kit that physicians liked to use with new patients. There were no generic versions of the kit—a niche that OWP would target. It found a US manufacturer with an ANDA (abbreviated new drug application) for lamotrigine. That meant the FDA had already approved the medicine that went *in* the bottle, but they also had to approve the name that went *on* the bottle.

"To get a brand name through the FDA," Bruce explains, "you have to have a study done by an outside consultant to see if your submission is valid. It's a complete scam in my opinion. You have to hire these guys—many of whom are former FDA employees—for $10,000 to look at your name and say, 'Yes, the FDA should approve it. Here's the report that says so.' When we did this for our lamotrigine product, we got a report indicating our name, 'Lamarow,' would be approved. We loved the name because it had R-O-W in it. But eighteen months later, when we were ready to manufacture and officially submitted Lamarow to the FDA, they rejected it. They had recently approved another drug with a similar name."

It would take at least six months to submit another name and get it approved. What could they do in the meantime? After much discussion they decided to sell a generic starter kit until they could get their own brand name approved. Their only competition would be the original drug, Lamictal, which was more expensive and no longer advertised by its maker.

By early 2018 the sales staff was rehired and expanded. After two weeks of training they went to work selling the starter kits. Orders started to come in, and OWP became cash flow positive for the first time. The second name submitted for lamotrigine, Subvenite, finally won FDA approval. Subvenite Starter Kits were ordered and began to ship in July 2018. Subvenite, not Roweepra, would be the foundation upon which OWP's future would be built.

An even more seismic problem surfaced than the ones OWP had with VCs and the FDA. Customers weren't buying enough product.

"The pharmaceutical market is very bizarre," Bruce

reflects. "I was taught in business to find out who's your customer. Who are you selling to? That's the person who pays you. In any other industry that makes sense. But we never talk to our customer. We deal 100 percent with the doctors. We have to sell the doctors, but they don't pay us or use our product. It's pharmacists who have to fill the doctor's prescription, but we don't sell to them either. And we don't really sell to patients, who finally get our product. They usually just have a small copay. Insurance companies or the government pay the rest.

"The breakdown in this chain for us came with the pharmacists," Bruce continues. "A doctor may write a prescription for Keppra, the brand-name version of levetiracetam. But when the patient takes it to a pharmacist, he or she may say, 'Your insurance says I have to fill this with a generic.' But there are seventeen or more companies that manufacture the generic. Pharmacists in the major chains are told to push their wholesaler's preferred generics. That's where the chains make their money. Even when a doctor has written specifically for our drug, many pharmacists won't honor this because it means making less profit. This practice is one reason our model didn't work like we'd expected."

Plan A, B, and C

"Entrepreneurs need to have a Plan A, a Plan B, a Plan C, and a Plan D," Scott insists. "You can't fall in love with Plan A. If it's not working, you've got to be brutally honest and make very tough business decisions incredibly fast. You have to shift to the next proposed pathway to profitability or you're dead. In our case, the pressure from the venture capital fund forced us to Plan B a lot faster than anticipated. Fortunately, we had a Plan B, and it worked."

This ability to pivot is key to survival. "In most cases, startups fail because the founders get so stuck on their original idea, they want to do everything in their power to prove it can work," writes Nicolas Cole in his article "Why Do Most Startups Fail?"

> What happens then is the founders feel married to the original idea. If you spend $2M on a marketing campaign, only to realize half-way through your product has some major flaws and you need to pivot, you're going to have to admit (to the world you've just advertised to) that you're changing the direction of the company.
>
> Many founders see this as a blow to their ego—and would rather try to make the original broken idea work, than admit they didn't have it all figured out and keep pivoting in a better direction.[68]

"I've been in business since the mid '70s and worked with a lot of business owners," says Scott's Halftime coach, Jim Dean. "Scott's different from most owners and entrepreneurs in many respects. To have a career the length of his and never having been part of a startup, then stepping out to create something new, that's extremely unusual. Having the courage to do that, and then sticking with it and working through all the challenges and uncertainties with a startup—again, that's pretty unusual. It takes a very dedicated and faithful guy to be able to stick with it. It's an incredible journey he's been on."

"*The race is not always to the swift,*" says inventor Richard C. Levy, "*but to those who keep running.* It is a mistake to think anything is made overnight, other than baked goods and newspapers." Levy's first corollary is *Nothing is as easy as it looks*. Levy's second corollary is *Everything takes longer than you think*.⁶⁹

OWP could add its own corollary: failure is part of the prescription for success.

And there's nothing like success to inspire imitation—something Scott had in mind from the beginning.

10
Social Entrepreneurs

Social entrepreneurship describes a set of behaviors that are exceptional. These behaviors should be encouraged and rewarded in those who have the capabilities and temperament for this kind of work. We could use many more of them.
—Gregory Dees

More than two hundred years ago, French economist Jean-Baptiste Say defined an *entrepreneur* as "someone who takes resources from a state of lower to a state of higher yield and productivity." Investopedia defines a *social entrepreneur* as "a person who pursues novel applications that have the potential to solve community-based problems. These individuals are willing to take on the risk and effort to create positive changes in society through their initiatives."[70]

Few people know more about social entrepreneurs than the late Bob Buford, former chairman of Buford Television. His social ventures included Leadership Network, The Peter F. Drucker Foundation for Nonprofit Management, and Halftime Institute, which helps business and professional leaders like Scott Boyer "move from success to significance."

Buford identified several trends influencing a new generation of social entrepreneurs. He called the first the AOL opportunity: A being affluence, O being options, and L being longevity. "Affluence" allows many people at a certain point in life to do something other than income-producing work. The options available have been increased by the demographic and economic changes in the Western world. And life expectancy ("longevity") has extended from around fifty in 1900 to around eighty in our time. People are not only living longer but they are healthier and more engaged in their senior years than previous generations.

One motivation for social entrepreneurs is seeing the shallowness of a materialistic value system and switching to a value system calibrated to serving others. "The form this service takes for each person usually grows out of something that has been in their life a long, long time," Buford observed. "One reason for the tremendous impact of the latest class of social entrepreneurs is that they're not leaving behind their business skill-sets when they cross over to the social sector. They see a social or spiritual opportunity and organize themselves in a businesslike way to address the challenge."[71]

Buford's example and writings had a profound influence on Scott, as noted in chapter 3. Scott arrived at midlife—halftime—having been successful but wanting to do something significant with his second half. He was encouraged not to abandon a lifetime of business experience and jump into the nonprofit sector. He was also encouraged *not* to stay put and just give away more money.

What he and his like-minded companions did was start a different kind of social enterprise (SE). A social enterprise is an organization that applies commercial strategies to maximize improvements in financial, social, and environmental well-being.

SE 1.0 and 2.0

Many businesses today are committed to doing more than creating profits for founders, paychecks for employees, and dividends for stockholders. One hears buzzwords like "conscious capitalism" and sees labels like "B Corps" that certify a business meets standards of social and environmental performance, accountability, and transparency.

A popular form of social enterprise is starting businesses to provide jobs and training to disadvantaged youth or to improve local communities. But Jim Schorr, a leading expert in social entrepreneurship, points out that most of these efforts fail because the businesses aren't large enough to survive long-term.

Another approach is where a for-profit company commits to a certain level of charitable giving to favorite causes, or sets up a not-for-profit foundation of its own. Most larger companies have some form of corporate giving. Charity Navigator reports that US corporations gave $20.77 billion in 2017 (5 percent of all donations). The downside of this approach is that funding can dry up if the business does poorly or the economy takes a downturn.

A third model of social enterprise is the "sell one, give one" arrangement where products, rather than cash, are given in direct proportion to sales. One leading example of this approach is TOMS Shoes. Blake Mycoskie started the company in 2006 with a One for One business model. Over the next decade TOMS donated 70 million pairs of shoes to needy children and branched out to other products, such as eyewear, coffee, and bags.

In 2014, Mycoskie sold 50 percent of TOMS to Bain Capital for $300 million. The company was bought out by investors in 2019 and now donates $1 for every $3 spent. But the sale exposes a vulnerability of this model. While the new owners may promise to maintain the philosophy of the founder, they can cut back or end the philanthropic program if they want. Or they can sell their shares to another investor, who may have no interest in the charitable component.

These three approaches could be called Social Enterprise 1.0 (SE 1.0). A less common but more viable social enterprise model could be called Social Enterprise 2.0 (SE 2.0). It features a for-profit business and a charitable foundation whose symbiotic partnership takes social enterprise to the next level.

The example that inspired Scott and Bruce was Tyndale House Enterprises. It's composed of Tyndale House Publishers, started in 1962 by Kenneth and Margaret Taylor, and Tyndale House Foundation, established a year later. In 2001, the Taylors transferred ownership of the for-profit business to the foundation. Dividends from the publishing company go to fund the philanthropy of the foundation.

A second example of SE 2.0 is the Lundbeck Pharmaceuticals Company and the Lundbeck Foundation in Denmark. Hans Lundbeck started the company in 1915, and the foundation was created by his widow in 1954. In 1999 the company went public, and the Lundbeck Foundation became the majority owner, with 70 percent of the stock. It has kept the business from being bought by one of the Pharma giants for its revenues, a healthy $2.8 billion in 2020.

This ownership arrangement makes it very difficult for the company to be sold out from under the foundation or to be acquired in a hostile takeover as happened with the Anheuser-Busch brewing company. A family business founded by immigrants after the Civil War, Anheuser-Busch went on to become the largest brewer in the world by revenue at the start of the twenty-first century. This made it an attractive target for a Belgium conglomerate, which executed a hostile takeover in 2008 at the cost of $46.5 billion. It was the largest cash acquisition in history at the time. August A. Busch and his son, August Busch IV, got almost half a billion dollars between them, while thousands of employees got pink slips.

   Being bought out is one way to lose control. Selling out is another. Selling a successful company for a sizable profit is often the exit strategy of choice, but it can leave the foundation high and dry once the founders are out of the picture. The SE 2.0 model guards against either outcome by having the not-for-profit foundation be the majority equity holder in the for-profit business.

   The SE 2.0 business is committed to making money, but that's not the primary reason for its existence. "All businesses exist to serve by increasing wealth," writes Kevin McCarthy in *Chief Leadership Officer*. "Increasing wealth matters in the larger social construct. Of the other sectors of society (for example, the arts, health, the environment, education, family, and government), the business sector generates the financial wealth that typically funds the others. Because increasing the wealth or the well-being of our society is our broadest duty, it is easy to get hyper-focused on the money part and leave out the people elements. Such a narrow or incomplete understanding of business as just 'making money' handicaps the strategy and business model."[72]

OWP and ROW were conjoined from birth so that profits from the business would fund the foundation's mission for the long haul. "Most startup pharmaceutical companies are funded by venture capital partners," Scott notes. "The typical plan is to build the company to a certain size and then sell it to a larger company. OWP is currently owned by myself and Bruce and a group of angel investors. We agreed going into the venture to donate or sell a majority stake of OWP to ROW, giving it a non-voting majority position and legal standing as a key stakeholder. We have structured our stock in a way to protect this relationship."

There are some challenges facing social entrepreneurs whatever structure they choose. In a 2018 article for the World Economic Forum, Kyle Zimmer and Kristine Pearson identify several obstacles hindering social sector entrepreneurs, including inconsistent access to capital, complex agendas, non-transparent reporting, and burnout of leaders. The OWP/ROW model manages to avoid or minimize these. It isn't dependent on outside capital. It generates what it needs for operations and grants. Its agenda is straightforward: sell quality meds in the US and make grants of medications and funds for equipment and training in underdeveloped areas. Its financials are public. Its leaders are energized by their work and want to stay involved as long as possible.

Sustainable and Scalable

"Adopting a mission to create and sustain social value is what distinguishes social entrepreneurs from business entrepreneurs," said the late Gregory Dees, director of the Center for the Advancement of Social Entrepreneurship at Duke. "For a social entrepreneur, the social mission is fundamental. This is a mission of social improvement that cannot be reduced to creating private benefits for individuals. . . . Social entrepreneurs look for a long-term social return on investment. They want more than a quick hit; they want to create lasting improvements. They think about sustaining the impact."[73]

Intent and implementation are two different things, however. When well-meaning people start not-for-profit organizations (NFPs) to do social good, they dedicate their time, energy, and resources to impact their areas of concern. But inconsistent cash flow can doom them to failure. Governments and foundations are the primary funding channels for NFPs. But governments either don't consistently fund NFPs, or they do so on a limited basis. And only a few foundations are self-sustaining. Most depend on constant fundraising.

This unpredictability of income undercuts the survivability of NFPs, as Jim Schorr notes: "Unless these organizations develop new models that enable social enterprises to deliver double bottom line results, or find permanent funding subsidies for their activities, their chances of long-term survival are not good. Most social purpose businesses lose money and require ongoing funding subsidies to support their operations. Unfortunately, these subsidies are not readily available."[74]

Sustainability and scalability were especially important to Scott: "We needed a sustainable way to help educate, diagnose, and treat people with epilepsy. We couldn't start a treatment plan and then tell patients we'd run out of money and therefore run out of medication. This would actually create more problems for them. If we'd set up a traditional NFP, we would always be chasing donations. We needed a consistent revenue stream to support a sustainable solution, and we needed it to be scalable because we were tackling a global issue."

Where are sustainable and scalable resources to be found? In the business world, as Michael Porter from Harvard explained in his TED talk "The Case for Letting Business Solve Social Problems": "What's the fundamental problem we have in dealing with these social problems? . . . Why is that? Because we don't have the resources. . . . If it's fundamentally a resource problem, where are the resources in society? How are those resources really created; the resources we're going to need to deal with all these societal challenges? I think the answer is very clear: They're in business."[75]

"We can harness the power of business to generate the dollars needed to impact social issues," Scott agrees. "As OWP succeeds as a business, it provides an ongoing source of revenue for ROW. We can make a positive difference for millions of epilepsy sufferers around the world."

"Until this opportunity with Scott came up, epilepsy rarely crossed my mind," Bruce admits. "I had no driving passion to help epilepsy patients. While this is a noble goal, it's not what drew me into this venture. What I do have is a passion for finding ways to harness the free-market capitalist system to do good for people. That's why I'm very passionate about the model we've put together. It allows people to do well while doing good in a way that's sustainable and scalable. I hope as we go forward, we will serve as an example to entrepreneurs in other sectors to build companies that will promote the well-being of humanity."

Indeed, many business leaders are looking for ways to use their skills and experiences not only to make a living but to make the world better. Scott adds a caveat, though: "It's best to build this into your organizational DNA from the beginning. Restructuring an existing for-profit enterprise to accomplish such goals would be very difficult. But if you start a business, you can structure it in a way that provides a sustainable and scalable solution to a social need you care about."

Leading by example is one reason Scott was invited in 2016 to be the Entrepreneur-in-Residence at North Central College in Naperville, Illinois, as a part of their new Center for Innovation and Entrepreneurship (CIE). CIE connects students and alumni with resources, mentoring, funding, and contacts to community entrepreneurs as they launch and grow their businesses. "Students of all majors need to know how to take an idea and run with it: Turn it into a project, fundraise for it, run a business," says Martha Carney, the Center's executive director. "This type of program can help increase the ROI on their education."[76]

Scott had worked with Martha before she started at North Central College. She approached him with the idea of OWP being an anchor company for their incubator. They wanted an established business that would take a significant portion of the office space they owned near the college. OWP wound up leasing about 3,000 square feet. Part of the expectation was that the company would hire interns, which it did. Some have become full-time employees.

Scott spoke on campus and in classes about not-for-profits in general and the OWP model in particular. In the spring he gave a TEDx talk at North Central, titled "The New Frontier of Social Enterprise." He looked at the evolution of social enterprise from not-for-profit foundations to new social enterprises that have the ability to sustain their business and scale their operations to accomplish their mission. A prime example: OWP and ROW.

In the summer of 2018, OWP moved to larger quarters

from the space they had rented from North Central. "We came out with new products," says Paul, wearing his COO hat for OWP. "We had Lamotrigine starter kits, Subvenite starter kits, and Subvenite maintenance dosages. We were more established in the market and needed to increase our sales force. By 2019 we had a dozen internal staff with some outsourced sales support as well.

"We worked with a company called InVentiv (now Syneos)," Paul expands. "They specialized in commercializing pharmaceutical products and provided us with Neuroscience Account Managers or NAMs. But when sales didn't take off fast enough, we had to drop the contract with Syneos and rely on our inside sales force. When sales picked up, we went back to Syneos and again contracted NAMs. Just before the [COVID-19] pandemic hit, we had dropped that contract again because our inside sales force was generating as much sales as the NAMs. We shifted more resources into provisioning our inside staff better. We increased our ability to do virtual presentations. And then the pandemic struck. By mid-March we started working remotely, along with the rest of the country. Our people could work from anywhere. We found we could do so many things virtually, like meeting with physicians, which has become a big part of how we operate now."

When OWP started bringing people back into the office in January 2021, the staff numbered fifteen. People observed physical distancing, wore masks, and had staggered schedules. "We found that although it's possible to work remotely, we're more effective when we work together. There is tremendous synergy and innovation that happens when you talk over the cubicle wall or pop your head into an office to ask a question. And now everybody has received full vaccination."

Given the new products OWP plans to roll out by the end of 2022, Paul projects a workforce of forty to forty-five by then.

Social Injustice

Social entrepreneurs are moved to action by the inequities and social injustices they see. They focus their intellect and energies on ways to right these wrongs. Their passion gives birth to original organizations and practical programs that others can buy into. Part of what prompted Scott to launch a high-risk startup was the injustice inherent in how Big Pharma marketed vital medications—or didn't market them—in much of the world because there's no money in it.

At least half of the world's population is too poor to access essential health-care services, according to reports by the UN and the World Economic Forum. Health-care expenses are also pushing hundreds of millions of people into poverty. A realistic solution to this crisis is suggested by Ellen Goodman and Meera Patel with Ashoka, the largest network of social entrepreneurs worldwide: "If we are going to tackle the global health crisis, we need to look beyond the narrow roles of the state, business and patients to draw on our collective strengths, and social entrepreneurship may just hold the key."[77]

Scott's sense of justice is informed by his faith. His Christian worldview has been shaped by the Bible, the church, and personal experience. He had met Bruce and Mark at church. Bruce and Paul had started a church together, and Paul knew Lori from church. Christian leaders like Bob Buford at Halftime and the speakers at the Global Leadership Summit (GLS) at Willow Creek Church had equipped and motivated Scott to live for a higher purpose.

Bruce has just as strong a spiritual motivation, as does

Paul. But they all agreed from the outset that faith would not be a litmus test for staff or a prerequisite for service. People would be hired based on their competency for the job. Philanthropy around the world would be based on need, not religion.

"I don't believe Christian executives should use their positions as platforms from which to preach to their employees or peers," says Buford. "Rather, they should share through the example of their lives. If executives would simply follow two rules, they would have plenty of opportunities to demonstrate the difference Christian belief makes. Rule one, don't duck; rule two, don't impose."

Amanda Award
Lisa and Mitch

"Our epilepsy journey began when my daughter Amanda had her first seizure at age three," says Lisa. After trying multiple therapies, her seizures proved intractable. Shortly after her eighth birthday, Amanda died from SUDEP (sudden unexpected death in epilepsy). Through the many challenges, we always felt supported by the doctors, nurses, teachers, and therapists who provided a community of care.

"Years later, I began to search for a nonprofit that helped children like Amanda in countries lacking the resources that had been available to us. The search led us to the ROW Foundation. As a business owner, my husband was particularly impressed with the OWP/ROW business model, which demonstrated a commitment to their mission. ROW was poised to provide seizure control to people who may not even have known that treatment is available. No one else was doing this.

"We went on to support ROW programs in India and

Zambia that bring hope to those who have difficulty accessing care. Partnering with ROW is our way to honor Amanda's memory. What an amazing opportunity it is to bring this hope to others—the hope of seizure control, as we had wanted for Amanda."

In 2019, ROW launched the Amanda Award to honor the memory of Amanda Brooke de los Santos, who passed away from seizures at a young age. Each year, ROW awards a grant to an organization with a track record of achieving meaningful results in addressing the epilepsy treatment gap.

11
Looking Ahead

*We make a living by what we get,
but we make a life by what we give.*
—Anonymous

Scott has never been to Armenia, or Haiti, or Kenya, or Sierra Leone, or many other countries where children and adults with epilepsy are being given new hope because of OWP and ROW. But what is happening in these far-off places fills his sails every day. "I wake up with incredible enthusiasm and motivation. I may be exhausted at times working six days a week, sometimes seven, but I'm very excited about what we're doing.

"OWP is no longer in the vulnerable position of a startup," Scott explains. "At this point, we are considered pretty stable. As part of getting a business loan, we met what's known as the ESG criteria. ESG stands for *environmental*, *social*, and *governance*. These standards are used by socially conscious investors to evaluate potential investments.

Expert trader and investment adviser James Chen explains the initials ESG: "Environmental criteria consider how a company performs as a steward of nature. Social criteria examine how it manages relationships with employees, suppliers, customers, and the communities where it operates. Governance deals with a company's leadership, executive pay, audits, internal controls, and shareholder rights."[78]

"We're a commercial, viable, profitable organization," Scott says. "We have people showing up at our doorstep all the time now who want to license our drugs in the US and places like Brazil and Germany. They're here because we are becoming the premier neuroscience child and adolescent pharmaceutical company in the country. I have no doubt that will happen."

ROW is also well established. As of the time of this writing, the foundation has made more than $20 million in medication and monetary grants in thirty countries. As OWP becomes more profitable, ROW could become the largest funder of projects serving people with epilepsy and associated psychiatric disorders in the world.

Scott agrees. "I have no question we will become the largest foundation focused on epilepsy and neuroscience disorders serving the under-resourced. There are other organizations focusing on neuroscience that do a lot of research, which is appropriate and important. But not a lot of foundations are actually getting medication and education and diagnostic equipment to the under-resourced around the world. And certainly not on the scale ROW will achieve.

"I'm a few years older than my dad, who had a fatal heart attack at fifty-eight," Scott reflects. "He worked very hard but didn't get to enjoy all he had accomplished. I've worked really hard to stay healthy. This has helped me cope with the physical and mental stress, of which there's been a lot. I want to be around to be part of OWP and ROW, but also to get this model out there as another option for people."

And like all savvy businessmen, Scott has an exit strategy.

Exit Strategy

Investopedia defines a *business exit strategy* as "an entrepreneur's strategic plan to sell his or her ownership in a company. . . . [It] gives a business owner a way to reduce or liquidate his stake in a business and, if the business is successful, make a substantial profit."[79]

When it comes to OWP, Scott never intends to sell the company. "That's not why we built it,'" he insists. "In fact, it's structured in such a way that it would be almost impossible to do. Neither my children, nor Bruce's, will have any significant equity in the company, so it won't happen after we're gone either." Nor does Scott plan to "make a substantial profit." "Bruce and I own the majority of the company," he says. "If we weren't incredibly disciplined and committed to this calling, there are so many opportunities to take a big chunk of money and sell the model down the river in exchange for the easy life."

Even before OWP became profitable, Scott and Ruth drafted a Founder's Pledge that puts a lifetime cap on what they will make from OWP.

The idea of a Founders Pledge is influenced by the Giving Pledge created in 2010 by Bill and Melinda Gates and Warren Buffett. It is a "global, multi-generational initiative designed to help address society's most pressing problems by encouraging the wealthiest individuals and families to give the majority of their wealth to philanthropic causes."[80]

Although aimed at the wealthy, the pledge is inspired by the example of millions of regular people who give generously and sacrificially to make the world better.

The Boyers' Pledge was written in 2017:

> My wife Ruth and I put our hearts and souls and time and money into starting OWP Pharmaceuticals. This was a leap of faith, but not a blind jump. We have sound business reasons to believe that our missional model will be very successful. As founders, we will benefit from OWP's success. Even before that becomes a reality we want to publicly state our intent not to let riches become a goal in our lives.
>
> We believe in "wealth" as a proper reward for a life well invested, just as an abundant crop is the natural reward for a diligent farmer. But we are not interested in "riches" as horded resources, or zeros in a bank account, or a way to keep score.
>
> We have drawn a line between what wealth and riches mean to us and put a number on it. We pledge that everything we earn through our involvement and investment in OWP over that number will be given to charity. As the business does well, we will use our profits to assist others who have not had the incredible opportunities or undeserved blessings we have enjoyed.
>
> We hope our commitment will help the investors, employees, and beneficiaries of OWP Pharmaceuticals remember that we exist, not to enrich a few but to empower the many.

"When you hear the word *wealth*, you shouldn't automatically go to personal wealth," Scott says. "There are such things as community wealth, country wealth, and global wealth. When you get to a certain point, it shouldn't be personal wealth you're working toward but more global wealth. For me, that's through ROW. A lot of people with epilepsy who get treated and have their seizures reduced or eliminated can now get jobs and do all sorts of things they couldn't before. Their human potential is released and improves the wealth of their communities, countries, and the world.

"I was talking recently with a friend in Big Pharma who would love to be involved with OWP. I asked how much was enough for him when it came to personal wealth. He gave me a number and I really didn't care how much it was. I was more interested that he had a definite point beyond which he would give everything else away. The kind of people I want at OWP are those who have drawn a line somewhere. If they just want as much personal wealth as they can get, they should go work for Merck or Pfizer or Bristol."

Bruce and Scott have talked about some options for when they cross their own personal wealth lines. In addition to giving to ROW, they might start a social capital fund to help others who have a worthy calling they are willing to work for so they wouldn't be reliant on venture capital or private equity. "Once you go down that path, which is 95 percent of the time," Scott warns, "the game is over. It's just a timing issue."

One of Scott's concerns is not letting money create family problems. "Too much money can screw up future generations," he believes. "Our kids and grandkids should have a reason to get up and go to work. We can help with their lifestyle, but we don't want to create a situation where they don't have to work for the rest of their lives. Hard work to create a situation where they don't have to work for the rest of their lives. Hard work and innovation are good for the soul. If we have the capacity to work, we should be working."

This concern is well founded. In his book *What Your Money Means (And How to Use It Well)*, Frank J. Hanna explains the difference between the fundamentals and non-essential wealth: "The fundamentals provide all the things money can buy to ensure that persons develop as they ought and become as productive as they can be. . . . The money that remains unspent after the fundamentals have been paid for is what we call non-essential wealth."

Hanna warns of the dangers of passing on nonessential wealth to the next generation: "Money can seriously damage those who receive it, particularly when those people are young and come into wealth before their characters have been formed. . . . If we can provide the fundamentals to another person, that's great. But to do more—to give them non-essential wealth—may well be the worst thing we could do for them. All we're adding to their lives is danger."[81]

In the Meantime . . .

As far as the immediate future, none of OWP's leadership is going anywhere. "I will definitely keep going for the next several years and see what happens," says the founder and CEO. "I'd like to work shorter hours, though. At our old building I used to come in on weekends to vacuum and dust and restock the drinks and snacks. I don't have to clean the bathrooms anymore, which is good. I've been able to hand off some of my responsibilities for daily business and focus on future development.

"Stephen helped us with some very important tasks," Scott says, "from arbitrating with the VC Fund to developing an effective board. He has tremendous experience and was a great chairman.

As far as other leadership roles, Scott knows he won't

be able to personally evaluate and approve all hires as in the early days. "I will have to assume those we hire are sold on our hybrid model. But you know what, we're starting to look like Pharma, we smell like Pharma, we quack like Pharma, so a lot people will think, 'Hey, pharmaceuticals. I know the industry and the pay is good.' We will need such professionals, but I want the people we hire to be here because of our model and what ROW is doing."

Scott adds a caveat for senior leadership: "For the people at the top, I really have to make sure they are aligned with our mission. I will ask them the same question I asked my friend about personal wealth: How much is enough? I don't care if they say $10 million, or $15 million, or $20 million; I just want an answer. I will show them my Founder's Pledge and ask them to do something similar. If that's a deal breaker, it's a deal breaker. If they can't put a number down they can live with, then they're not aligned with our mission and I won't hire them."

Cofounder Bruce Duncan plans to continue as CFO for several more years. "I really enjoy what I'm doing," he says. "And actually getting a salary is nice."

Because of rapid growth in 2018, OWP asked Paul Regan to bring his expertise back to the business side of the equation. He assumed the role of COO and handed ROW's day-to-day operations to Ken Koskela and Lori Hairrell. "When OWP fills the COO position with someone more permanent, I'm anxious to resume as ROW's president. I want to expand our programs and relationships with organizations around the world. I love being part of the brain trust that's putting it all together. At some point I would step back from the presidency but still work actively with ROW into my early seventies. I love what we're doing and want to stay involved as long as I can."

All three men are in agreement as to what corporate growth might look like in the near future. OWP will stay centered on epilepsy and associated psychiatric disorders. But they would also like to replicate its model for other diseases and conditions. One way they might do this would be to start separate divisions or LLCs for other markets. These entities could have their own products and staffs and humanitarian causes. They could seek outside investors, but OWP would always hold a controlling interest.

"Right now we're focusing on neuroscience," Bruce says. "Could we go into oncology or cardiovascular? Absolutely. I expect OWP to branch into other medical fields. And hopefully we will inspire entrepreneurs in other fields to adopt our model. It can work for almost any new business that has a clear vision and can create a reasonably strong cash flow."

Serving as an inspiration to others was always a part of OWP's founding vision. Early on Scott wrote in his blog:

> My challenge to you is to pick a cause and start thinking about how to use this unique model to create a sustainable way to positively impact it. It doesn't matter if you are young or old. It actually may be easier when you are at either bookend of your professional life. Are you willing to step into the unknown? What are your areas of training or expertise? What is your area of passion? What is your calling or cause you want to impact? When are you going to do something about it? As William James once said: "Act as if what you do makes a difference. It does."

Drug Test Answers

1. The average life span in the US in 1900 was forty-nine. The average life span in 2020, after discoveries such as vaccines, insulin, penicillin, and beta-blockers, is _79_.[82]

2. Without this drug, penicillin, 75 percent of the people now alive would not be alive because their parents or grandparents would have died from infections.[83]

3. How big is the worldwide pharmaceutical industry in US dollars? Approximately $1.3 trillion[84]

4. _88_ percent of the global pharmaceutical market is focused on the US, Europe, and Asia.[85]

5. Americans spend more on prescription drugs than anyone else in the world, about $1,200 per person annually.[86]

6. _55_ percent of Americans take prescription meds.[87]

7. According to Gallup's ratings of US Business and Industry in 2020, which sectors are held in the lowest esteem by Americans?
Sports industry: trust ranking of −10
Pharmaceutical industry: trust ranking of −15
Federal government: trust ranking of −20[88]

8. Generic drugs are used to fill __90__ percent of prescriptions in the US. Are these generics readily available in low- and middle-income countries? __No__ [89]

9. __2__ billion people living in low- and middle-income countries do not have access to modern medicine.[90]

10. Around __50__ million people have epilepsy, with more than __5 million__ new cases every year.[91]

Appendix

Epilepsy: A Public Health Imperative
World Health Organization

(The following materials are direct quotations. Abridged by Ken Koskela.)

DEFINITIONS AND CAUSES OF EPILEPSY

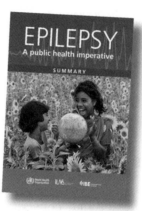

- Epilepsy is a brain disease characterized by an enduring predisposition to generate epileptic seizures. (page 3)
- Epilepsy is a brain disease characterized by abnormal brain activity causing seizures or unusual behaviour, sensations and sometimes loss of awareness. (page xiii)
- ILAE definition: A brain disease defined by any of the following conditions: (page 3)
  - at least two unprovoked (or reflex) seizures occurring > 24 hours apart;
  - one unprovoked (or reflex) seizure and a probability of further seizures similar to the general recurrence risk (at least 60%) after two unprovoked seizures, occurring over the next 10 years;
  - diagnosis of an epilepsy syndrome
- Epilepsy has a variety of causes, ranging from

genetic, metabolic, infectious, structural, immune and unknown. (page xiv)

PREVALENCE AND BURDEN OF EPILEPSY GLOBALLY
Prevalence
- ◆ Epilepsy is one of the most common neurological diseases and affects people of all ages, races, social classes and geographical locations. (page 13)
- ◆ With around 50 million people affected worldwide and more than 5 million new cases every year, epilepsy is one of the most common chronic neurological conditions. (page 110)
- ◆ More than 5 million new cases are diagnosed every year and the number of people with epilepsy is expected to increase further. (page 2)
- ◆ Around 7.6 per 1000 persons have epilepsy during their lifetime. (page xiv)

Burden
- ◆ It carries neurological, cognitive, psychological and social consequences and accounts for a significant proportion of the world's burden of disease. (Preface, page vi)
- ◆ It accounts for 0.5% of the global burden of disease and affects people of all ages living in countries of all income levels. (page 110)
- ◆ It accounted for over 13 million disability-adjusted life years (DALYs; a summary measure of health loss defined by the sum of years of life lost for premature mortality and years lived with disability) in 2016 or 0.5% of the overall global burden of disease. (page 2)
- ◆ Major gaps in awareness, diagnosis and treatment are

devastating the lives of millions of people with epilepsy throughout the world. (page 2)

EPILEPSY SHOULD BE A GLOBAL PRIORITY

- ◆ If we are to achieve the health-related Sustainable Development Goals (SDGs), it is imperative that we substantially scale up global efforts to address epilepsy. (Foreword, page v)
- ◆ At the Sixty-Eighth World Health Assembly (WHA) in 2015, 194 Member States unanimously adopted resolution WHA68.20 on epilepsy which called for the need for coordinated action at the country level to address its health, social and public knowledge implications. (page xiii)

EPILEPSY IS USUALLY TREATABLE AND OFTEN PREVENTABLE

- ◆ People with epilepsy, their families, and the community need to be aware that seizures can be stopped. Seizure control requires the correct diagnosis, initiation of appropriate treatment for the epilepsy and comorbidities, and careful follow-up, with the ultimate aim of suppressing seizures and improving quality of life. (page 36)
- ◆ Epilepsy is a treatable condition. Up to 70% of people with epilepsy could become seizure free with appropriate diagnosis and use of cost-effective, and commonly available, antiseizure medicines. This can lead people with epilepsy to continue, or return to, a full and productive life. (page xiv)
- ◆ An estimated 25% of epilepsy cases are preventable. The major modifiable risk factors for epilepsy are:

perinatal insults, central nervous system infections, traumatic brain injury and stroke. (page xii)

HIGHER PREVALENCE IN LOW- AND MIDDLE-INCOME COUNTRIES

- ◆ There is a higher incidence of epilepsy in low- and middle-income countries (LMIC) (139 per 100 000 person-years) compared with high-income countries (HIC) (48.9). (page xiv)
- ◆ Nearly 80% of those with epilepsy reside in LMIC, where rates of epilepsy prevalence and incidence are higher than in HIC. (page 10)
- ◆ The differences in rates of epilepsy are likely due to the causes of disease in these settings, including endemic infections (e.g. malaria or neurocysticercosis), higher incidence of injuries (e.g. related to motor vehicle accidents and birth), as well as lack of access to health care. (page 10)

THE EPILEPSY TREATMENT GAP IN LOW- AND MIDDLE-INCOME COUNTRIES

- ◆ The epilepsy treatment gap is defined as the proportion of people with epilepsy who require treatment but do not receive it, expressed as a percentage. (page 2)
- ◆ We know that while 80% of people with epilepsy live in low- and middle-income countries, most of them do not have access to treatment. This is despite the availability of effective antiseizure medicines, which can cost as little as US$ 5 per year. (Foreword, page v)

- Three-quarters of people living with epilepsy in low-income countries do not get the treatment they need. Yet, up to 70% of people with epilepsy could become seizure free with appropriate use of cost effective antiseizure medicines. (page xi)
- Nearly 80% of people with epilepsy live in LMIC, where treatment gaps exceed 75% in most low-income countries and 50% in most middle-income countries. This is despite the effectiveness and low cost of antiseizure medicines. (page xiii)
- Estimates of the treatment gap in low-income countries is over 75%, and tend to be higher in rural versus urban areas. (page 52)
- Numerous drivers of the global treatment gap have been identified, including inadequate access to trained professionals, diagnostics, transportation and health care facilities; sociocultural factors including stigmatization, awareness and acceptability of treatment; as well as poor availability and non-affordability of medicines. (page 52)
- Sustained access to antiseizure medicines is a major barrier to treatment in LMIC. (page 52)
- A lack of action to address the epilepsy treatment gap has dire consequences for people's lives and well-being, and impacts social and economic development. (Foreword, page v)

CONSEQUENCES OF UNTREATED EPILEPSY—OVERALL

- Epilepsy has a high risk of disability, psychiatric comorbidity, social isolation and premature death. (Preface, page vi)
- The physical, psychological and social consequences

of epilepsy impose significant burdens on people living with the condition and their families. Around the world, people with epilepsy and their families suffer from stigma and discrimination, often facing serious difficulties in education, employment, marriage and reproduction. (page xiii)
- ◆ People with epilepsy often encounter barriers in achieving their full potential due to unmet needs in the areas of civil rights, education, employment, residential and community services, and access to appropriate and affordable health care. (page 20)
- ◆ Its impact may be due to the physical and psychological consequences of seizures; the social exclusion faced by individuals and their families; and the stigma, as children may be barred from school, and adults may be banned from marriage, driving and employment. (page 13)
- ◆ The suffering and disability caused by epilepsy place a huge burden not only on individuals with epilepsy, but also on their families and indirectly on the community. (page 13)

CONSEQUENCES OF UNTREATED EPILEPSY—PHYSICAL

- ◆ The risk of premature death in people with epilepsy is up to three times that of the general population. (page xi)
- ◆ Epilepsy carries an overall increased risk of premature mortality. SUDEP, status epilepticus, accidents, drowning, unintentional injuries and suicide are the most important and potentially preventable causes of death in people with epilepsy. (page 2)

BURDEN OF EPILEPSY ON PERSONS WITH EPILEPSY—COMORBIDITIES

- ◆ Roughly half of the people with epilepsy have coexisting physical or psychiatric conditions. (page xiv)
- ◆ Physical and psychiatric comorbidities in people with epilepsy are associated with poorer health outcomes, increased health care needs, decreased quality of life and greater social exclusion. (page xiv)
- ◆ Psychiatric comorbidities are the most prevalent comorbidities with a reported prevalence of 29–40%, which is 7- to 10-fold higher than that of mental health conditions in the general population. (page 15)
- ◆ The most prevalent psychiatric comorbidities were depression (23.1%) and anxiety (20.2%), as compared with 4.4% and 3.6% in the general population globally. (page 15)
- ◆ Alcohol abuse (8.7%), drug abuse (7.8%) and interictal psychosis (5.2%) are less prevalent psychiatric comorbidities in epilepsy. (page 15)
- ◆ Attempted and completed suicides are estimated to occur in 5–14.3% of people with epilepsy. (page 15)

COMORBIDITIES IN CHILDREN

- ◆ Due to the significance of birth injuries as a cause of childhood epilepsy, as high as 70% of children with epilepsy have a comorbidity. (page 16)
- ◆ Intellectual disability is the most common comorbidity in children with epilepsy (30–40%). (page xiv)
- ◆ The most common psychiatric/behavioural disorders among children who have epilepsy include autism spectrum disorder (ASD), attention deficit hyperactivity disorder (ADHD), depressive and anxiety disorders.

(page 16)
- ◆ The prevalence of ADHD is estimated to be between 12% and 39% in children with epilepsy and is much higher than the 3–7% in the general population of children. (page 16)
- ◆ Emotional disorders can be found in about 16% of children with epilepsy compared with 4.2% in the general population. (page 16)

CONSEQUENCES OF UNTREATED EPILEPSY—ECONOMIC

- ◆ A systematic review showed people with epilepsy had lower employment rates as compared with the general population in all continents. (page 74)
- ◆ Epilepsy has significant economic implications in terms of health care needs and lost productivity at work. (page xi)
- ◆ Epilepsy is often related to conditions of poverty, and epilepsy results in poverty from lost earnings due to disability, time seeking care, and stigma around employability. This affects people with epilepsy as well as family members, especially those caring for children with epilepsy. (page 2)
- ◆ Many individuals with epilepsy report that stigma poses a barrier to employment and leads to fear, embarrassment, rejection and hostility by others at the workplace. (page 74)

CONSEQUENCES OF UNTREATED EPILEPSY—SOCIAL / STIGMA

- ◆ Left untreated, people living with epilepsy face devastating social consequences, including stigma, discrimination and human rights violations. (page xiv)
- ◆ People with epilepsy and their families can be the

target of discrimination and human rights violations, affecting their quality of life and social inclusion, which often dissuades them from seeking treatment. (page 2)
- Globally, stigmatized people with epilepsy are more likely to have lower self-esteem and quality of life, greater social isolation, poorer psychological health and worse epilepsy control. (page 72)
- Many children with epilepsy do not go to school; adults are denied work, the right to drive or marriage. (Preface, page vi)
- This includes the perception of epilepsy as a form of insanity, ruining people's lives, and being untreatable or contagious. (page xvii)
- Institutionalized discrimination in epilepsy affects employment, education, marriage and childbearing, and driving regulations. (page xvii)
- People with epilepsy and their families may be confronted with social ostracism and outright discrimination in part due to misconceptions that have existed for centuries. (page 70)
- The ILAE/IBE survey (Annex 1) identified three prevalent misconceptions that can fuel stigma in epilepsy: people with epilepsy are contagious, crazy and possessed by demons, bewitched or punished by gods. (page 70)
- These misconceptions can perpetuate stigma and can lead to social isolation, delays in seeking treatment and care, unemployment, poverty and poor mental health in people with epilepsy. (page 68)
- Misconceptions contribute to the burden of illness in epilepsy and lead to stigma. They cause people with

epilepsy to feel shame, embarrassment and disgrace. (page 71)
- The emotional impact of feeling socially excluded contributes to the physical, psychological and social burden of epilepsy. (page 71)
- Stigma can delay appropriate health seeking, access to care, health financing and availability of treatment. (page 71)
- In areas where the perceived cause of epilepsy is widely associated with witchcraft or demonic possession, care seeking is directed toward traditional healers rather than hospital or clinic based healing. (page 72)
- The burden of stigma, however, is greatest for people who live in low-income, less developed settings, and for this reason, stigma contributes to social and economic morbidity. (page 72)
- In fearing contamination or alienation from others, families may banish the person with epilepsy from the community to live as outcasts or force them to live in separate sleeping quarters away from the rest of the household. (page 72)
- Unmarried adult females are vulnerable to sexual exploitation, physical abuse and extreme poverty. (page 72)
- Stigmatization and discrimination lead to worsening of psychological well-being, resulting in greater stigmatization than experienced before. (page 74)
- Stigma is associated with higher levels of depression and anxiety. (page 75)
- In addition to personal impact, the family and care partners of people with epilepsy also experience increased burden and stress, and poorer family functioning. (page 75)

EXAMPLES BY GEOGRAPHIC CONTEXT
- In many Asian and African cultures, females with epilepsy are viewed as poor wives: unable to properly take care of children, cook on a fire or contribute to household chores. (page 72)
- In a study from Zambia, sexual assault rates for women with epilepsy were 20% versus 3% among women with other chronic conditions. (page 72)
- Women with epilepsy in Nigeria face multiple social and economic challenges with one-third victimized with physical abuse from members of their household and 10% reporting sexual assault. (page 72)
- In the United Republic of Tanzania, youth with epilepsy were more likely to experience adverse employment, educational and relationship outcomes in the transition to adult life, with the greatest disadvantage experienced by females. (page 72)

HIGHER CONSEQUENCES OF EPILEPSY IN LOW- AND MIDDLE-INCOME COUNTRIES
- Unfortunately, the areas with the highest burden of epilepsy are often those with the lowest coverage of health services. (page 2)
- Epilepsy in LMIC carries a significantly higher mortality, as in HIC. In LMIC the excess mortality is associated with lack of access to health facilities and preventable causes. (page 10)
- There is a higher incidence of epilepsy in LMIC compared with HIC, 139.0 (95% CI: 69.4–278.2) and 48.9 (95% CI: 39.0–61.1), respectively. (page 11)
- Epilepsy in LMIC carries a significantly greater mortality than in HIC. In LMICs the excess mortality is more likely to be associated with causes

attributable to lack of access to health facilities such as status epilepticus, and preventable causes such as drowning, head injuries, and burns. (page 14)
- ◆ The incidence of epilepsy is also higher in the lower socioeconomic classes in HIC, and, within the same population, people of differing ethnic origin. (page 11)
- ◆ In population-based studies in HIC, SMR calculations (i.e. the ratio between deaths in people with epilepsy and deaths expected in the general population) are 1.6 to 3.0 (page 14)
- ◆ The burden is greatest in LMIC, where nearly 80% of people with epilepsy live: in low-income countries three-quarters of people do not receive the treatment they need. (page 110)

ADDRESSING THE TREATMENT GAP

- ◆ It is feasible to integrate epilepsy treatment into primary health care—training nonspecialist providers, investing in continuous supplies of antiseizure medicines and strengthening health systems can substantially reduce the epilepsy treatment gap. (page xi)
- ◆ A significant proportion of the burden of epilepsy could be avoided by scaling up routine availability of antiseizure medicines, possible at an annual cost as low as US$ 5 per person. (page xi)
- ◆ Improving knowledge and raising awareness of epilepsy in schools, work places, and communities is needed to reduce stigma. (page xi)
- ◆ Identifying and dispelling the misconceptions that cause stigma is a first step to reducing stigma. (page 68)

IMPORTANCE OF A SUSTAINABLE SUPPLY OF TREATMENT MEDICATION

- Many essential antiseizure medicines are not readily available in several regions, particularly in the public sector, and the price of these medicines in low-income countries is several times higher compared with HIC. (page 24)
- Ensuring uninterrupted supply of appropriate access to antiseizure medicines is one of the highest priorities. (page xvii)
- Access to antiseizure medicines offers the potential for approximately 70% of people with epilepsy to live seizure free (on medicines), with an opportunity to impact their quality of life and participation in society. (page xvii)
- An abrupt withdrawal of antiseizure medicines can have life-threatening consequences, including status epilepticus. Therefore, it is essential to ensure that access to these medicines is sustained over time to permit uninterrupted treatment. (page 52)

The 171-page report can be downloaded at: https://www.who.int/publications/i/item/epilepsy-a-public-health-imperative.

Working Toward One World. One Standard.

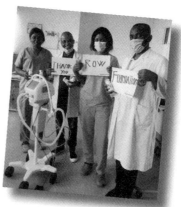

The ROW Foundation provides treatment resources, including the antiseizure drugs Roweepra and Subvenite from OWP Pharmaceuticals, to people with epilepsy and associated psychiatric disorders. ROW is also actively helping to address stigma, provide opportunities for training, and improve diagnosis.

ROW has worked with partners in these locations:
Armenia
Bolivia
Cameroon
Democratic Republic of Congo
Ethiopia
Gambia
Ghana
Grenada
Guinea

Guyana
Haiti
India
Kenya
Liberia
Malawi
Nigeria
Pakistan
Palestinian Territories
Puerto Rico
Republic of Georgia
Sierra Leone
Sudan
Suriname
Syria
Tanzania
Uganda
United States
Venezuela
Zambia
Zimbabwe

ROW has partnered with a wide range of organizations:
Americares
Arabkir United Children's Charity Foundation
Armenia Artsakh Foundation
Armenian American Pharmacists' Association
Armenian League Against Epilepsy
ASLEK Epilepsy Foundation
Boston Children's Hospital
Cameroon Baptist Convention Health Services
Children's Hope
Christian Medical and Dental Associations

CLIDEP Epilepsy Clinic
Concerned Haitian-Americans of Illinois (CHAI)
Cuatro Por Venezuela
CURE International
Dalhousie University
Direct Relief
Edward Francis Small Teaching Hospital
Emmanuel Hospital Association - US
Epilepsy Alliance North Carolina
Epilepsy Association of Zambia
Epilepsy Awareness Uganda
Epilepsy Foundation Guyana
Epilepsy Foundation of Greater Chicago
Epilepsy Foundation of North Carolina
Epilepsy Foundation of North Central Illinois, Iowa and Nebraska
Epilepsy Health Management
Epilepsy Medicare Foundation
Foundation for People with Epilepsy
Georgian League Against Epilepsy
Global Organization of Health Education
Grenada General Hospital
Guiding Light Orphans
Healey International Relief Foundation
Hôpital Provincial General de Référence de Bukavu
International League Against Epilepsy
Janjay Village of Hope, Inc.
Kifafa Care and Support Child Project
Kiserem Epilepsy Foundation
La Maison Santé Global
Loma Linda University Health
Massachusetts General Hospital
Medical Assistance Sierra Leone

Pretola Global Health and Consulting
Provision Charitable Foundation
Purple Bench Initiative
Rachael K Foundation
Santokba Durlabhji Memorial Hospital
Save Haven Community Services
Solidarity Bridge
St. Vincentius Hospital
Syrian American Medical Society (SAMS)
TeleEEG
UTH Children's Hospital
West Atlantic Brain & Stroke Foundation
World Medical Relief
Yale University

Endnotes

Introduction

1. Deyan Georgiev, *Small Business Statistics [Guide to Success in 2020]* (blog), Review 42, July 4, 2021, https://review42.com/resources/small-business-statistics/.
2. The Harris Poll, "Harris Poll: Only Nine Percent of U.S. Consumers Believe Pharma and Biotechnology Put Patients over Profits; Only 16 Percent Believe Health Insurers Do," accessed June 21, 2021, https://theharrispoll.com/only-nine-percent-of-u-s-consumers-believe-pharmaceutical-and-biotechnology-companies-put-patients-over-profits-while-only-16-percent-believe-health-insurance-companies-do-according-to-a-harris-pol/.
3. George W. Merck, quoted in Robert F. Bruner et. al, *The Portable MBA*, 4th ed. (Hoboken, NJ: Wiley & Sons, 2003), 56.

Chapter 1

4. Arthur A. Daemmrich and Mary Ellen Bowden, "Emergence of Pharmaceutical Science and Industry: 1870–1930," *Chemical and Engineering News*, June 20, 2005, http://pubsapp.acs.org/cen/coverstory/83/8325/8325emergence.html.
5. Eric Sagonowsky, "The Top 20 Pharma Companies by 2020 Revenue," *Fierce Pharma*, March 29, 2021, https://www.fiercepharma.com/special-report/top-20-pharma-companies-by-2020-revenue.

6. Manuchair S. Ebadi, *Desk Reference of Clinical Pharmacology*, 2nd ed. (Boca Raton, FL: CRC Press, 2008), 1.
7. Robin Walsh, "A History of the Pharmaceutical Industry," *Pharmaphorum*, September 1, 2020, https://pharmaphorum.com/articles/a_history_of_the_pharmaceutical_industry/.
8. Stewart Lawrence, "Vaccinations Have Saved More Than 10 Million Lives Since 1962," *Study Foods*, February 5, 2021, https://www.studyfinds.org/vaccinations-save-lives-vaccines-study-finds/.
9. Walter Isaacson, *The Code Breaker: Jennifer Doudna, Gene Editing, and the Future of the Human Race* (New York: Simon & Schuster, 2021), 447.
10. Isaacson, 447.
11. Walsh, "A History of the Pharmaceutical Industry."
12. "Global Biotechnology Market: 4 Pivotal Trends Expected to Augment the Industry Size Through 2025," *BioSpace*, January 5, 2021, https://www.biospace.com/article/global-biotechnology-market-4-pivotal-trends-expected-to-augment-the-industry-size-through-2025/.
13. Meghana Keshavan, "Big Biotech Is Here—and It's Starting to Look a Lot Like Big Pharma," *STAT*, June 6, 2016, https://www.statnews.com/2016/06/06/big-biotech-pharma/.
14. U.S. Food & Drug Administration, "Generic Drugs: Questions & Answers," FDA.gov, March 16, 2021, https://www.fda.gov/drugs/questions-answers/generic-drugs-questions-answers.
15. "Global Generic Drugs Market to Reach US$ 517 Billion by 2026, Catalyzed by Increasing Prevalence of Chronic Diseases," IMARC Group, June 14, 2019, https://www.imarcgroup.com/growth-in-the-generic-drug-market.

16. Carolyn Y. Johnson, "The Generic Drug Industry Has Brought Huge Cost Savings. That May Be Changing," *Washington Post*, August 1, 2017, https://www.washingtonpost.com/business/economy/the-generic-drug-industry-has-brought-huge-cost-savings-that-may-be-changing/2017/08/01/ee128d0a-68cf-11e7-8eb5-cb-ccc2e7bfbf_story.html.
17. Walsh, "A History of the Pharmaceutical Industry."

Chapter 2

18. Keith Speights, "12 Big Pharma Stats That Will Blow You Away," Motley Fool, October 4, 2018, https://www.fool.com/investing/2016/07/31/12-big-pharma-stats-that-will-blow-you-away.aspx.
19. *The Pharmaceutical Industry and Global Health: Facts and Figures 2021* (Geneva: International Federation of Pharmaceutical Manufacturers & Associations, 2021), foreword, https://www.ifpma.org/wp-content/uploads/2021/04/IFPMA-Facts-And-Figures-2021.pdf.
20. Daniel J. DeNoon, "The 10 Most Important Drugs," WebMD, accessed May 1, 2021, https://www.webmd.com/genital-herpes/features/10-most-important-drugs.
21. Crescent B. Martin et al., "Prescription Drug Use in the United States, 2015–2016," *NCHS Data Brief*, no. 334 (May 2019), https://stacks.cdc.gov/view/cdc/78184.
22. Am J Health, "National Trends in Prescription Drug Expenditures and Projections for 2020," PubMed.gov, July 23, 2020, https://pubmed.ncbi.nlm.nih.gov/32412055/.
23. Gallup, "Business and Industry Sector Ratings," Gallup.com, July 30–August 12, 2020, https://news.gallup.com/poll/12748/business-industry-sector-ratings.aspx.

24. Michael Gibney and Kris Elaine Figuracion, "Cancer Drugs Show Big Sales Rise in 2020; AbbVie's Humira Again Tops List," *S&P Global Market Intelligence*, March 22, 2021, https://www.spglobal.com/marketintelligence/en/news-insights/latest-news-headlines/cancer-drugs-show-big-sales-rise-in-2020-abbvie-s-humira-again-tops-list-63249898.

25. Brian Buntz, "GSK, Pfizer and J&J Among the Most-Fined Drug Companies, According to Study," *Pharmaceutical Processing World*, November 18, 2020, https://www.pharmaceuticalprocessingworld.com/gsk-pfizer-and-jj-among-the-most-fined-drug-companies-according-to-study/.

26. Erin Duffin, "Leading Lobbying Industries in the United States in 2020, by Total Lobbying Spending," Statista, March 4, 2021, https://www.statista.com/statistics/257364/top-lobbying-industries-in-the-us/.

27. Sammy Almashat, Sidney M. Wolfe, and Michael Carome, "Twenty-Five Years of Pharmaceutical Industry Criminal and Civil Penalties: 1991 Through 2015," *Public Citizen*, March 31, 2016, https://www.citizen.org/wp-content/uploads/migration/2311.pdf.

28. Martin Shkreli, "I Would've Raised Prices Higher," *Forbes*, December 3, 2015, https://www.forbes.com/video/4644635141001/#5e56fb911017.

29. David Crow, "Pharma Chief Defends 400% Drug Price Rise as a 'Moral Requirement,'" *Financial Times*, September 11, 2018, https://www.ft.com/content/48b0ce2c-b544-11e8-bbc3-ccd7de085ffe.

30. Brad Tuttle, "Why the EpiPen Price Scandal Sums Up Everything We Hate About Big Business & Politics," *Time*, September 21, 2016, https://time.com/4502891/epipen-pricing-scandal-big-pharma-politics/.

31. Aaron Berman et al, "Curbing Unfair Drug Prices: A Primer for States," Yale Global Health Justice Partnership, August 2017, https://law.yale.edu/sites/default/files/area/center/ghjp/documents/curbing_unfair_drug_prices-policy_paper-080717.pdf.
32. Ethan Rome, "Big Pharma Pockets $711 Billion in Profits by Robbing Seniors, Taxpayers," HuffPost, April 8, 2013, updated December 06, 2017, https://www.huffingtonpost.com/entry/big-pharma-pockets-711-bi_b_3034525.html.
33. Kenneth L. Davis, "Big Pharma Has Broken Its Social Contract: How to Restore Fairness in Drug Pricing," *Forbes*, November 1, 2016, https://www.forbes.com/sites/kennethdavis/2016/11/01/big-pharma-has-broken-its-social-contract-how-to-restore-fairness-in-drug-pricing/#28df96522aa9.
34. David Lazarus, "Big Pharma Really, Really Doesn't Want You to Know the True Value of Its Drugs," *Los Angeles Times*, February 17, 2017, https://www.latimes.com/business/lazarus/la-fi-lazarus-drug-pricing-evzio-20170217-story.html.
35. Lazarus.
36. Tim Wu, "How to Stop Drug Price Gouging, *New York Times*, April 20, 2017, https://www.nytimes.com/2017/04/20/opinion/how-to-stop-drug-price-gouging.html.
37. Chuck Carnevale, "The Top 3 Medical Distributors Are On Sale: AmerisourceBergen, Cardinal Health and McKesson Corp.," Seeking Alpha, January 31, 2020, https://seekingalpha.com/article/4320481-top-3-medical-distributors-are-on-sale-amerisourcebergen-cardinal-health-and-mckesson-corp.
38. Rebecca Pifer, "PhRMA, Hospital War over Drug Prices Heats Up," *Biopharma Dive*, September 6, 2018,

https://www.biopharmadive.com/news/phrma-hospital-war-over-drug-prices-heats-up/531756/.
39. Washington Post Staff, "The Opioid Files," *Washington Post*, January 24, 2020, https://www.washingtonpost.com/national/2019/07/20/opioid-files/?arc404=true.
40. Merck, in Bruner et. al, *The Portable MBA*, 56 (see intro., n. 3).
41. Davis, "Big Pharma Has Broken Its Social Contract."

Chapter 3

42. Allie Nawrat, "Stop Ignoring the Two Billion: Pharma's Role in Expanding Access to Medicine," *Pharma Technology*, accessed January 20, 2020. https://www.pharmaceutical-technology.com/features/access-to-medicine-pharma/
43. "New Study from the Foundation Analyses 10 Years of Data on Pharma Companies and Access to Medicine," Access to Medicine Foundation website, May 16, 2019, https://accesstomedicinefoundation.org/news/new-study-from-the-foundation-analyses-10-years-of-data-on-pharma-companies-and-access-to-medicine.
44. Bob Buford, quoted in Merrill J. Oster and Mike Hamel, *Giving Back: Using Your Influence to Create Social Change* (Colorado Springs, CO: NavPress, 2003), 14.
45. Herman Cain, quoted in Bill Thrall, Bruce McNicol, and Ken McElrath, *The Ascent of a Leader: How Ordinary Relationships Develop Extraordinary Character and Influence* (San Francisco: Jossey-Bass, 1999), 149.

Chapter 4

46. Harriet Rubin, "Peter's Principles," *Inc.*, March 1, 1998, https://www.inc.com/magazine/19980301/887.html.

47. Jim Collins and Jerry I. Porras, *Built to Last: Successful Habits of Visionary Companies*, 3rd ed. (New York: HarperBusiness, 2011), 229–30. Italics in original.
48. Jim Collins, "The Foundation for Doing Good," *Inc.*, December 1, 1997, https://www.inc.com/magazine/19971201/1378.html.

Chapter 5
49. Johnson, "The Generic Drug Industry Has Brought Huge Cost Savings" (see chap. 1, n. 16).
50. "Values, Vision & Mission," OWP Pharmaceuticals, Inc. website, accessed June 22, 2021, https://owppharma.com/faqs/
51. David Ficker, "Epilepsy Comorbidities," Epilepsy Foundation, March 2015, https://www.epilepsy.com/living-epilepsy/epilepsy-and/professional-health-care-providers/joint-content-partnership-aes/epilepsy-comorbidities.

Chapter 6
52. "Epilepsy: Key Facts," World Health Organization website, June 20, 2019, https://www.who.int/news-room/fact-sheets/detail/epilepsy.
53. "Epilepsy: Key Facts."
54. Athanasios Covanis et al., "From Global Campaign to Global Commitment: The World Health Assembly's Resolution on Epilepsy," *Epilepsia* 56, no. 11 (2015): 1651–57, https://pubmed.ncbi.nlm.nih.gov/26391429/.
55. "WHO Resolution Calls for Integrated Action on Epilepsy and Other Neurological Disorders," World Health Organization, November 13, 2020, https://www.who.int/news/item/13-11-2020-wha-resolution-calls-for-integrated-action-on-epilepsy-and-other-neurological-disorders.

56. Matthew M. Zack and Rosemarie Kobau, "National and State Estimates of the Numbers of Adults and Children with Active Epilepsy—United States, 2015," CDC, August 11, 2017, https://www.cdc.gov/mmwr/volumes/66/wr/mm6631a1.htm?s_cid=mm6631a1_e&utm_content=bufferd1ca5&utm_medium=social&utm_source=facebook.com&utm_campaign=buffer.
57. Diane Patternak, quoted in Elizabeth Shimer Bowers, "Overcoming the Stigma of Epilepsy," *Everyday Health*, June 28, 2013, https://www.everydayhealth.com/epilepsy/overcoming-the-stigma-of-epilepsy.aspx.
58. Orrin Devinsky, quoted in Aliyah Baruchin, "Battling Epilepsy and Its Stigma," *New York Times*, February 20, 2007, http://www.nytimes.com/2007/02/20/health/20epil.html?pagewanted=all&_r=0.
59. Ilo E. Leppik, "The Place of Levetiracetam in the Treatment of Epilepsy," *Epilepsia* 42, Suppl. 4 (2001): 44, https://onlinelibrary.wiley.com/doi/epdf/10.1111/j.1528-1167.2001.00010.x.
60. "Effectiveness of Treatment," Epilepsy Foundation Greater Chicago, https://epilepsychicago.org/what-is-epilepsy/treatment/effectiveness-of-treatment/.
61. "MDS-3: Managing Access to Medicines and Health Technologies (Third Edition)," Kumarian Press, 2013, https://digicollections.net/medicinedocs/documents/s19577en/s19577en.pdf.
62. Research and Markets, "World Epilepsy Drugs Market and Global Epilepsy Drugs Competitor Market Share Scenario 2020–2027," PR Newswire, March 12, 2021, https://www.prnewswire.com/news-releases/world-epilepsy-drugs-market-and-global-epilepsy-drugs-competitor-market-share-scenario-2020-2027-301246381.html.

Chapter 7

63. See Simon Sinek, "Inspire Your People," simonsinek.com, https://simonsinek.com/commit/.
64. Julie Rawe, "Where Does Your Gift Go?" *Time*, October 28, 2001, http://content.time.com/time/magazine/article/0,9171,181602,00.html.
65. "Human Rights and Health," World Health Organization, December 29, 2017, https://www.who.int/news-room/fact-sheets/detail/human-rights-and-health.

Chapter 8

66. See The Lion's Den website, https://see.thelionsden.us/.

Chapter 9

67. Nicolás Cerdeira, Kyril Kotashev, "Startup Failure Rate: Ultimate Report + Infographic [2021]," Failory, March 25, 2021, https://www.failory.com/blog/startup-failure-rate.
68. Nicolas Cole, "Why Do Most Startups Fail? Because Founders Get Stuck Making This 1 Shameful Mistake," *Inc.*, February 9, 2018, https://www.inc.com/nicolas-cole/the-majority-of-startups-fail-heres-why-thats-a-founder-problem-not-a-startup-problem.html.
69. Richard C. Levy, *The Complete Idiot's Guide to Cashing In on Your Invention*, 2nd ed. (New York: Penguin, 2010), 12.

Chapter 10

70. Adam Hayes, "Social Entrepreneur," Investopedia, April 24, 2021, https://www.investopedia.com/terms/s/social-entrepreneur.asp.
71. Mike Hamel and Merrill Oster, *The Entrepreneur's Creed: The Principles & Passions of 20 Successful*

Entrepreneurs (Nashville, TN: B & H Publishing, 2001).

72. Kevin W. McCarthy, *Chief Leadership Officer: Increasing Wealth So Everyone Profits* (Grandview, MO: On-Purpose Publishing, 2017), 36, 38.

73. J. Gregory Dees, "The Meaning of 'Social Entrepreneurship,'" Duke University, original draft: October 31, 1998, revised: May 30, 2001, https://centers.fuqua.duke.edu/case/wp-content/uploads/sites/7/2015/03/Article_Dees_MeaningofSocialEntrepreneurship_2001.pdf.

74. Jim Schorr, "Social Enterprise 2.0: Moving Toward a Sustainable Model," *Stanford Social Innovation Review*, Summer 2006, https://community-wealth.org/sites/clone.community-wealth.org/files/downloads/article-schorr.pdf.

75. Michael Porter, "The Case for Letting Business Solve Social Problems," TEDGlobal, 2013, https://www.ted.com/talks/michael_porter_why_business_can_be_good_at_solving_social_problems/transcript.

76. "North Central Launches Its Own Startup: New Center for Innovation and Entrepreneurship (CIE)," North Central College website, May 2, 2016, https://www.northcentralcollege.edu/news/2016/05/02/north-central-launches-its-own-startup-new-center-innovation-and-entrepreneurship.

77. Ellen Goodman and Meera Patel, "Meet the Social Entrepreneurs Defining the Future of Healthcare," *HuffPost*, December 6, 2017, https://www.huffingtonpost.com/skoll-foundation/meet-the-social-entrepren_b_9708072.html.

Chapter 11

78. James Chen, "Environmental, Social, and Governance (ESG) Criteria," Investopedia, March 5, 2021, https://www.investopedia.com/terms/e/environmental-social-and-governance-esg-criteria.asp.
79. Adam Hayes, "Business Exit Strategy," Investopedia, updated November 1, 2020, https://www.investopedia.com/terms/b/business-exit-strategy.asp.
80. "Giving Pledge Welcomes 14 New Philanthropic Individuals and Couples," press release, givingpledge.org, May 30, 2017, https://givingpledge.org/PressRelease.aspx?date=05.30.2017.
81. Frank J. Hanna, *What Your Money Means (And How to Use It Well)* (Dallas: Crossroad, 2008), chap. 5, loc. 1224, Kindle.

Drug Test

82. "U.S. Life Expectancy 1950–2021," *Macrotrends*, accessed June 21, 2021, https://www.macrotrends.net/countries/USA/united-states/life-expectancy.
83. Peter Hogg, "Top 10 Most Important Drugs in History," *Proclinical*, January 6, 2016, https://www.proclinical.com/blogs/2016-6/top-10-most-important-drugs-in-history.
84. Matej Mikulic, "Pharmaceutical Market: Worldwide Revenue 2001–2020," Statista, May 4, 2021, https://www.statista.com/statistics/263102/pharmaceutical-market-worldwide-revenue-since-2001/.
85. Ljubica Cvetkovska, "38 Fundamental Pharmaceutical Statistics and Facts for 2021," Supplements 101, April 2, 2021, https://supplements101.net/pharmaceutical-statistics/.

86. Robert Langreth, "Drug Prices," *Bloomberg*, September 16, 2020, https://www.bloomberg.com/quicktake/drug-prices.
87. Robert Preidt, "Americans Taking More Prescription Drugs Than Ever," WebMD, August 3, 2017, https://www.webmd.com/drug-medication/news/20170803/americans-taking-more-prescription-drugs-than-ever-survey.
88. "Business and Industry Sector Ratings," Gallup.com, July 30–August 12, 2020, https://news.gallup.com/poll/12748/business-industry-sector-ratings.aspx.
89. "2020 Generic Drug & Biosimilars Access and Savings in the U.S. Report," The Association for Accessible Medicines, accessiblemeds.org, accessed June 21, 2021, https://accessiblemeds.org/resources/reports/2020-generic-drug-biosimilars-access-and-savings-us-report.
90. Allie Nawrat, "Stop Ignoring the Two Billion: Pharma's Role in Expanding Access to Medicine," *Pharma Technology Focus*, accessed June 21, 2021, https://pharma.nridigital.com/pharma_feb20/stop_ignoring_the_two_billion_pharma_s_role_in_expanding_access_to_medicine.
91. "Epilepsy: Key Facts," WHO, June 20, 2019, https://www.who.int/news-room/fact-sheets/detail/epilepsy.

About the Dreamer

Scott Boyer's almost thirty years in the pharmaceutical industry included leading the sales and marketing efforts for numerous branded drugs for Abbott and Bristol-Myers Squibb. He left his lucrative career to found OWP  Pharmaceuticals and the ROW Foundation, driven by a passion to create a social enterprise model that provides the best level of medical and pharmaceutical care for all people regardless of who they are or where they live.

About the Author

Mike Hamel is a storyteller by trade and the author/editor of more than twenty nonfiction books on topics as wide-ranging as business, finance, political theory, health care, nonprofits, and religion. He has also written eighteen books for children and young adults.

Learn more on Amazon, https://www.amazon.com/Mike-Hamel/e/B001JSB7FE/ and Wikipedia, https://en.wikipedia.org/wiki/Mike_Hamel.

You can contact Mike at emtcom@comcast.net.